Praise for *Attitudes of Gratitude*

"We have spent the last decades trying to have what we want. This inspiring book shows us how to rejoice in what we have. Ryan proves that, no matter how worried we are about the future, feeling and expressing gratitude allows us to celebrate and deeply appreciate the privilege of being in the precious present. Ryan graciously shows that if we're going to 'have an attitude,' gratitude is the right one."

—PAUL PEARSALL, PH.D.
author of *The Pleasure Prescription* and *The Heart's Code*

"There is a powerful connection between being grateful, appreciating the gift of living well and happiness. M. J. Ryan's *Attitudes of Gratitude* reminds us that gratitude is an achievement and creates lasting happiness when we commit ourselves to this illuminated state of desire—mind and passionate 'spirit-energy' to live the best life possible."

—ALEXANDRA STODDARD
author of *Things Good Mothers Know* and *Choosing Happiness*

"Exquisitely reconnects us to the wonder and satisfaction that can be found in our daily lives."

"*Attitudes of Gratitude* is a most delightful feast of spiritual insights. The quotes at the beginning of each section are outstanding. The personal vignettes are deep yet written simply with the flow of love in each line. It is a book to be savored."

"Each section of *Attitudes of Gratitude* acts as a mini refresher course in the wisdom of focusing on what is really important."

"What M. J. Ryan has done for the world—and it's no small gift—is to forever connect gratitude with joy."

"The practice of gratitude is perhaps the most under-utilized way to grow spiritually. It is also the fastest way to connect with the joy of being alive. M. J. Ryan provides the inspiration, tools, and heartfelt stories to help anyone make gratitude a wonderful part of their daily life. Honesty and practical wisdom shine throughout the pages of this important book."

—JONATHAN ROBINSON
author of *Communication Miracles for Couples* and *Shortcuts to Bliss*

"For me, this book could not have come at a better time. I have been working on bringing the ancient practice of gratitude to life in my life and finding that making a list just wasn't enough. Here are hundreds of ways to soften and loosen, to celebrate and pause. Thank you, M. J. Ryan."

—JENNIFER LOUDEN
author of *The Woman's Comfort Book* and *The Woman's Retreat Book*

"Thanksgiving is one of the most exciting and power-ful antidotes to moral apathy and spiritual indiffer-ence available to human beings. The stories in this book testify to this wonderful value that all of us can practice—no matter our social, economic, cultural, or religious background. Gratitude is ours for the taking, but not to be taken for granted!"

—ELIZABETH ESPERSEN
executive director, Center for World Thanksgiving

"M. J. Ryan understands the human heart and how to release its power. *Attitudes of Gratitude* is a deeply touching and truly transforming guide for life."

—HUGH PRATHER
author of *Notes to Myself* and *The Little Book of Letting Go*

M. J. RYAN

Attitudes
OF
Gratitude

10TH ANNIVERSARY EDITION

How to Give and Receive Joy Every Day of Your Life

Conari Press

This edition first published in 2009 by
Red Wheel/Weiser, LLC
With offices at:
665 Third Street, Suite 400
San Francisco, CA 94107
www.redwheelweiser.com

ISBN: 978-1-57324-411-4

Library of Congress Cataloging-in-Publication Data available upon request.

Cover and text design by Sara Gillingham
Typeset in Archer and Gotham

Printed in Canada
MP
10 9 8 7 6 5 4 3

Life will bring you pain all by itself.
Your responsibility is to create joy.

—MILTON ERICKSON, M.D.

Contents

CHAPTER 3

The Attitudes of Gratitude 73

CHAPTER 4

The Practices of Gratitude 119

CHAPTER 5

The Deepening Journey 185

A Decade of Thankfulness

I can't believe it's been ten years since I wrote *Attitudes of Gratitude*. My daughter Ana, who features prominently as a baby in these pages, is now 11 and exhibiting all the pre-teen sighing over her mother's behavior. Fortunately, our family's practice of gratitude is firmly in place, which helps us stay connected to one another and to the blessings in our lives. A friend of Ana's was staying over recently and I told her to sit down for dinner. "I know," she sighed, "at your house, you have to eat a vegetable and you have to say one thing you're thankful for."

The world is also a very different place than it was ten years ago. One of the changes for the better is that gratitude has gone mainstream. When I sat down to write about gratefulness in 1999, the only books on the subject were religious ones and the scientific research was non-existent. So what I did was think deeply about the effects of giving thanks on myself and others and write about that. Since then, primarily because of the research of members

of the positive psychology movement, as well as
the book *The Secret,* which touted gratitude as the
key to grabbing all the goodies you could ever want,
there's been an explosion of writings.

I've watched it all with great interest, particularly in the research of David McCullough, Robert
Emmons, and David Snowdon. What they and others have discovered confirms all of my amateur
armchair philosophizing. So what you will read in
these pages is consistent with what we now know
from science. (More on that in a bit.)

I still think that gratitude is magic, not because
it will result in pink Priuses manifesting in our
driveways or millions of dollars in our mailboxes as
some of the *Secret* followers would have us believe.
It's because gratitude is one of the only totally free,
unbelievably simple ways to experience a sense of
well-being and contentment on an ongoing basis.
It's so easy that many of us still seem to discount it
as simplistic, or want to complicate it somehow.

I remember emailing back and forth with a
reporter a couple years ago. She kept sending me
questions about how to practice gratitude. I kept
writing back, in various forms, "Notice what's

right in your life." Finally, after the fourth or fifth question, I replied, "That's it. It's as simple as that! There's no magic formula about writing it down or thinking of ten things or putting the list under your pillow. However and wherever you choose to notice the goodness in your life, you will experience the uplift of gratefulness. It's because it's so simple that we can't believe it will work."

But you don't have to take my word for it anymore. Research has now confirmed the emotional and physical benefits of giving thanks. One of the most powerful studies comes from Martin Seligman's Reflective Happiness website. After counting their blessings for one week, 92 percent of people felt happier and 94 percent of people who said they were depressed felt less depressed. That means gratitude is as powerful as antidepressants and therapy. Now I'm not suggesting you throw away your medication. Just be sure to add this easy upper to your routine. In other studies, 90 percent of people found that expressing gratitude made them more joyful; 84 percent said it reduced stress and depression, and helped create optimism; and 78 percent said it gave them more energy.

Research also shows that being grateful means you'll take better care of yourself. Folks who kept a weekly gratitude journal had fewer physical problems and exercised more regularly, ate better and got regular checkups. It seems that when we recognize ourselves and our lives as the precious opportunities they truly are, we take better care of ourselves. It also makes us kinder and more generous to others, less materialistic, more forgiving, more able to deal with stress, and less prone to bitterness, envy, resentment, or greed. When you take all these good effects together, practicing appreciation adds 6.9 years to your life, which is greater statistically than stopping smoking or exercising.

What's going on here? Why is it that gratitude can have such positive mind/body/spirit effects? All we have so far is a hypothesis, but I believe it is a powerful one. From research done on Buddhist monks' brains, we are beginning to believe that when we think positive thoughts such as gratitude, kindness, optimism, etc., we activate our left pre-frontal cortex and flood our bodies with the feel-good hormones, which give us an upswing in mood in the short term and strengthens our immune system in the long run. Conversely, when we think negative, angry, worried, hopeless, pessimistic thoughts, we activate our right pre-frontal cortex and flood our body with the stress hormones, which send us into fight or flight, which depresses our mood and suppresses our immune system. In other words, we are bathing our bodies/minds/spirits in good or bad chemicals based on our thoughts. And gratitude is one of the most powerful positive chemical creators!

I could go on and on. If you are interested in the science, do be sure to read Robert Emmons' book, *Thanks*. I'd rather tell you a story that says it all. One day I got an email request from a guy who was a real estate agent in Southern California. He had started a non-profit helping teens in the California foster system who were about to turn eighteen and lose state support. His non-profit offers transition money and help. He wanted to know if I could sell him some copies of *Attitudes of Gratitude* at a discount to give away to people who donated to his charity. I arranged to give him some copies for free and promptly forgot all about it.

Some time later, a package arrived in my mailbox. When I opened it, a small rock fell out. I opened the accompanying letter. It was from the realtor, thanking me for the books and sending me the story of one of the youngsters he's helping, a seventeen-year-old named Lauren.

Lauren has lived in twelve different foster homes since she was eight. When she moves, her possessions fit in one plastic trash bag. She's about to "age out" of the California foster system, with no place to live, no money, and no job. But she's consistently happy. Why? Because when she was ten, she lived with Mommy Jean. Mommy Jean gave Lauren a small rock and told her to carry it always in her pocket. Each time she felt it, she was to think of something to be grateful for. Every day since, no matter where she lives, Lauren touches that rock and is grateful.

Since that day, whenever I speak about gratitude, I give out pebbles. If I could, I would give you one right now. Not only to help you practice an attitude of gratitude, but to help you remember, each time you touch it, that the amazing power of gratitude is available to you each and every day, no matter your circumstances.

—M. J. RYAN

INTRODUCTION

My Thanks

Since 1994, when I wrote *A Grateful Heart: Daily Blessings for the Evening Meal from Buddha to the Beatles*, I have been thinking and reading about gratitude, and wondering what else I could do to enhance my own sense of thankfulness on a daily level and support it in other people. Many people asked for a sequel to *A Grateful Heart*, but this time I wanted to do something different than a collection of prayers. And so *Attitudes of Gratitude* has been "cooking" in my soul for over four years, until Brenda Knight came along and suggested that I write about gratitude in the way you'll see here. Thank you, BK, for the inspiration and for several stories.

In this work, I have had many teachers, those who have blessed my life with their presence, and those whom I know only from the pages of their books. I thank first of all Dawna Markova for loving friendship and profound thinking on this (and every other) topic, as well as her inspiring embodiment of an asset focus. Her perspectives have become so much my own that it's hard to say where her thinking lets off and mine takes up. She recently spent a day with me, generously offering practices, stories, and perspectives to make this book more useful and less banal. It is a much better book for her contribution.

I also give my loving thanks to Daphne Rose Kingma, for first teaching me the effects of gratitude, for letting me quote from her many books, for imbuing my writing style through example by some of her poetry, and for writing the best thank you notes in the world; to Molly Fumia and Will Glennon, for thinking with me at various spots in the writing of this book; to Sue Patton Thoele, for friendship over the years and allowing me to quote from *The Woman's Book of Spirit*; to my editor Claudia Schaab, who pushed me at the end; and to poet Mark Nepo, for being so generous with his words. Finally, I thank Annette Madden for sharing stories and for being the most vivid example of an "attitude of gratitude" I know.

I also acknowledge Brother David Steindl-Rast, whose insightful writings and tapes on gratefulness, particularly *Gratefulness, the Heart of Prayer*, inform every page of this book; Lewis Smedes'

MY THANKS

A Pretty Good Person: What It Takes to Live with Courage, Gratitude, and Integrity; Adair Lara's *Slowing Down in a Speeded Up World*; David Kundtz's *Stopping: How to Be Still When You Have to Keep Going*; Sarah Ban Brethnach's *Simple Abundance*; Richard Louv's *The Web of Life*; "Positive Image, Positive Action," by David L. Cooperider; and Joan Borysenko's *Fire in the Soul: A New Psychology of Spiritual Optimism*. Thanks also to all the authors whose words I use as jumping-off points, and to the entire staff of Conari Press, who make this and all of our books happen. I consider it a great privilege to be able to create "books that make a difference" with you.

CHAPTER 1

The Simple Joy of Living from a Grateful Heart

If you look to others for fulfillment,
you will never truly be fulfilled.
If your happiness depends on money,
you will never be happy with yourself.
Be content with what you have;
rejoice in the way things are.
When you realize there is nothing lacking,
the whole world belongs to you.

—LAO TZU

Yesterday, while putting the final touches on this book, I went to lunch at a Chinese restaurant with my friend Annette to talk about gratitude. When I opened my fortune cookie at the end of the meal, the message was, "Stop searching. Happiness is just next to you." Talk about perfect timing! For that is exactly what this book is all about. Happiness, the sheer joy of being alive, is within our reach. All we need is an attitude of gratitude. Gratitude creates happiness because it makes us feel full, complete; gratitude is the realization that we have everything we need, at least in this moment.

There is a saying that people teach what they most need to learn, and nowhere is that more true than with me and gratitude. I wrote this book not only because I think gratitude is vitally important to our world, but because I want to become more consciously grateful myself. I do not set myself up as an "expert," but rather a person on a path like the rest of us, each of us becoming the fullness of who he or she is meant to be.

Like so many of us, I spent a great deal of my life, in my twenties and early thirties, cataloging all the ways I had been injured and abused. In therapy and out, with friends and loved ones, I analyzed and categorized the whos, whats, and wheres of my misery. I was a confirmed pessimist, always able to see the dark side of anything and everything. My belief was that life was hard and disaster was looming around every corner. If things were going well, it was only a matter of time before they would take a turn for the worse. Despite life's difficulties, it was my responsibility to do all the good I could and become the best person I could be. If I thought about gratitude at all, it was only to take a moment to give thanks for a few people in my life who had helped me feel loved.

Gradually, things changed for me. I can't point to a single event, a life-changing moment, when my attitudes suddenly transformed. Rather, slowly, as I came to understand my wounding better and began to heal, I started to notice the dearth of positive emotions in my life. I wasn't so miserable, worried, or alone anymore, but I knew precious little about joy, happiness, optimism, faith, and trust. So I began to study these emotions. (I always was a good student—give me something to study and I'll figure it out.)

I adopted certain people who seemed to naturally radiate happiness as my teachers of optimism and joyfulness. One of the things I noticed is that these people all had a profound sense of gratitude that seemed to flow uninhibitedly from them. Investigating further, I discovered that each of them had experienced at least as difficult an early life, if not more challenging, as I had. But my teachers consciously chose to adopt certain attitudes, such as gratitude, that led them to great happiness.

That's when I learned that you don't have to be saddled for life with the mental attitudes you adopted in early childhood. All of us are free to change our minds, and as we change our minds, our experiences will also change. So I set out on a course to be more grateful, joyful, and hopeful. The result of my course is what you are holding in your hands.

A few of my basic assumptions: I've learned over time that it helps to take the long view, to choose to see our lives from a spiritual perspective. I know we are here to "grow our souls," to heal our wounds—or at least bless our woundedness—and become more loving, kind, fearless, and hopeful. The longer I live, the more I recognize that cultivating an attitude

of gratitude is the key to living from an open heart, that is, living in a spirit of joyful expectation.

Gratitude is not just the key. It's a magic key—all you need to do is to use it, and the world is suddenly transformed into a beautiful wonderland, in which you are invited to play. That's because, like most of the great spiritual truths, gratitude is stunningly simple. This is not to say, however, that an attitude of gratitude is necessarily easy to practice. All kinds of distractions, obfuscation, and negative attitudes from our upbringings may get in the way. But all you really have to do is make a commitment to do it, and the magic will be yours.

One of the incredible truths about gratitude is that it is impossible to feel both the positive emotion of thankfulness and a negative emotion such as anger or fear at the same time. Gratitude births only positive feelings—love, compassion, joy, and hope. As we focus on what we are thankful for, fear, anger, and bitterness simply melt away, seemingly without effort.

How can this be? The answer is that gratitude helps us track success, to notice what is right in our lives, and the brain naturally works to track success.

If you have ever watched a baby learn something, you'll know what I mean. Learning to walk, for example, she stands and puts out one foot. Boom! Down she goes because her balance wasn't right. Instead of castigating herself for blowing it, getting angry, or blaming the floor or her shoe, she just registers that it didn't work because her foot was too far out and tries again. She just keeps trying and trying, discarding what doesn't work without obsessing on it, and incorporating what's right until she can walk. Fall, fall, fall, walk, fall, fall, walk, walk, walk!

As we get older, however, we get schooled in our mistakes, and learn to focus on what's not right, what is lacking, missing, inadequate, and painful. That's why gratitude is so powerful. It helps us to return to our natural state of joyfulness where we notice what's right instead of what's wrong. Gratitude reminds us to be like plants, which turn toward, not away, from the light.

Because of the simple power of gratitude, it's easy to make all kinds of Pollyanna-ish generalities, which slide off into meaninglessness and are boring to read about. My hope is that within these pages you'll find true inspiration and some solid ideas for making the practice of living from a grateful heart real and meaningful.

To entice, encourage, and support you in your commitment, this little book begins with The Gifts of Gratitude, which look at what happens in our lives when we begin to practice gratitude. Don't worry if you don't know how to do it yet. Right now, we are focusing on the wonderful effects your new attitudes will create. We then go to The Attitudes of Gratitude, which are the outlooks or stances we need to take in cultivating gratefulness. Finally we move to The Practices of Gratitude, which are the practical ways we can develop and maintain thankfulness in our daily lives.

In a sense, each of the sixty chapters is a meditation in and of itself. This is not a book to be read at one sitting. Rather, I encourage you to read one chapter and let it sink in for a while—a day, two days, even a week or longer—before moving onto the next. Since gratitude is both an attitude and a practice, you need time to integrate the learnings so they can become truly yours, and not something you just read, put away, and forget.

To get started, take a few minutes right now to reflect on a happy moment in your own life that stands out for you, a moment that stays with you, even if it happened ten, twenty, or forty years ago. Experience it again: see the scene, hear the sounds that were around you, feel the sensations. What was it about that moment that stays with you? Was gratitude a part of it? What was going on for you that allowed you to feel grateful?

For me it is tiny kittens crawling down my back when I was about two. I can feel the tiny claws, hear their little mewls, and see the grey wispy baby fur. It is the prickle of the tiny claws against my skin—the sensation so deliciously startling—that makes me smile even now. It's the first memory I have of the wonder of being alive in a body. It was the newness, the "first everness" that allowed me in that moment to feel grateful for being alive, and it is why that minute of my life continues to be one of my most powerful memories.

It has been a great joy for me to write this book, for its creation has been an act of gratitude in and of itself—for those who have so unselfishly taught

ATTITUDES OF GRATITUDE

and inspired me throughout my life; for those who shared specific ideas, stories, and practices with me; for my mind's ability to put it together; and for you, the reader, for being interested and willing to enter into the experience.

That's the most wonderful thing I've discovered so far about gratitude—it makes you feel full, bursting with delight, just to remember the gifts you have received. Thus are we doubly blessed when we receive something, for the gift itself, and later, in recall, for the miracle of having been given it.

CHAPTER 2

The Gifts of Gratitude

Gratitude unlocks the fullness of life. It turns what we have into enough, and more. It turns denial into acceptance, chaos into order, confusion to clarity.... Gratitude makes sense of our past, brings peace for today, and creates a vision for tomorrow.

—MELODY BEATTIE

Consciously cultivating thankfulness is a journey of the soul, one that begins when we look around us and see the positive effects that gratitude creates. We do this by noticing those around us to whom gratefulness comes easily and realize how much we enjoy being around these people. We also tap into these gifts as we think about times in the past when we felt particularly grateful. Remember the peacefulness and the delight that accompanied those times? As we come to understand the gifts of gratitude, we realize that being grateful is not something remote or foreign, but part of the natural joyful expression of our full humanness.

Gratitude Is the Mother of Joy

Joy is prayer—Joy is strength—Joy is love—Joy is a net of love by which you can catch souls. She gives most who gives with joy.

—MOTHER TERESA

I don't know about you, but in general, there hasn't been a lot of joy, that opening and swelling of the heart, in my life. It wasn't because of my circumstances, because they weren't particularly hard, but because of my mental training. Growing up, I learned to plan and to work hard. Accomplishments were good because they led somewhere I was planning to go: high school, college, a good job, a relationship. But they weren't to be relished and celebrated in and of themselves.

Like so many of us, I was so busy climbing the ladder of success, that I took no time to enjoy the journey. I was too busy getting on to the next challenge. When I think back on particular occasions for joy in my past—graduating valedictorian of my high school, getting married, making a bestseller list for *Random Acts of Kindness*, for example—I realize that as soon as I attained each goal, my eyes were immediately on the next "prize": getting to the top of my college class, having a baby, getting on the *New York Times* bestseller list. It was as if I was a machine, mindlessly churning out accomplishments and not stopping to relish the journey along the way.

But I got sick and tired of a joyless existence, and so have thought a lot in the past few years about how to bring more joy into my life. The more I think about it, the more I believe that joy and gratitude are inseparable. Joy is defined in the dictionary as an "emotion evoked by well-being, success, or good fortune or by the prospect of possessing what one desires," while gratitude is that "state of being appreciative of benefits received." In other words, whenever we are appreciative, we are filled with a sense of well-being and swept up by the feeling of joy.

So I determined to stop climbing mindlessly to some undefined peak of accomplishment and focus my attention on all the wonderful things that were happening in my day-to-day existence. As I do, without my even trying, joy creeps in.

How about you? As Sarah Ban Breathnach puts it, "Begin today. Declare out loud to the Universe that you are willing to let go of struggle and eager to learn through joy." Then think of all that you have accomplished today and celebrate each feat, no matter its size.

Gratitude Makes Us Young

The invariable mark of wisdom is to see
the miraculous in the common.

—RALPH WALDO EMERSON

Young children are such exuberant, joy-filled creatures, eager to embrace life in all its mystery and
majesty. Everything is new and exciting; everything—a bubble, a snowflake, a mud puddle—is a
gift. But something in the process of growing up
so often takes the juice out of us. We become
encrusted, hard, jaded. We lose our joy, our exu-
berance, our passionate embrace of life. We trudge
instead of skip, retreat instead of explore, "too old for
that," whatever "that" is.

This drying up is so common that when we meet
a vibrant, joy-filled older person, he or she stands
out as a singular exception. But we don't have to
lose the happiness or juiciness of youth. All we
need to do is to tap into our sense of gratitude, for
when we do, we are like little children again, seeing
the world for the first time.

In *Simple Pleasures of the Garden*, Dawna
Markova shares a story about such a woman:
"Several years ago, I was walking in March along a
gravel road that led to the ocean in Rhode Island.
A very old and thin woman came hobbling down a
driveway toward me. I waved and continued walking, but as I passed, she grabbed my arm, turned
around and began to pull me in the direction of her
house. I instantly thought of the witch in Hansel
and Gretel, and tried to pull back, but that only
made her clutch tighter around my wrist. Besides,
she didn't cackle, so I relented.

"She didn't say a word, in fact, until we
approached her house: a shingle-style cottage with
green shutters and a front lawn erupting everywhere in purple crocus. She released me there,
throwing her arms up in the air and shouting, 'Look
at this splendor! Isn't it a miracle?!'"

This old woman was open to the magic and
beauty of life, and her sparkling eyes and eagerness
to share made her and everything around her more
vibrant and alive.

Gratitude Makes Us Feel Good

*Mental sunshine will cause the flowers
of peace, happiness, and prosperity to
grow upon the face of the Earth. Be a
creator of mental sunshine.*

—GRAFFITI ON A WALL IN BERKELEY, CALIFORNIA

Tom comes from a family of highly successful busi-
nesspeople who taught him to climb the ladder of
success by criticizing him whenever he did something wrong. He learned early on that life is "hard
work," that it's a "dog-eat-dog world," and that to get
ahead he had to never make a mistake. While he
did succeed, including getting an M.B.A. from a top
business school, he was never happy. To him, work
seemed only drudgery; he spent much of his time
noticing what he did wrong: he didn't assert himself at the meeting, he should have made more calls.
Most of the time he felt lifeless and depressed.

Finally Tom went to a therapist to ask for a
prescription for Prozac. But since he really didn't
want to take an antidepressant if he didn't have
to, at the therapist's suggestion, he agreed to first

try something else for one month. Before he started work in the morning, he was to ask himself, "What do I feel grateful for about myself?" In this way, he reminded himself of his resources, strengths, and talents. Then, at the end of the day, he was to finish work by asking, "What did I do today that I feel good about?"

"Do you know what I discovered?" he told me. "Gratitude is a natural upper. It works so well that now, whenever I feel my energy going down during the day, I ask myself, what do I feel grateful for in this moment?" By concentrating on what he's doing right and what he appreciates about himself, Tom overcame his depression and has begun to look forward to work.

Gratitude makes us feel good because it helps us widen our frame of vision. Under depression or stress, we can develop tunnel vision, seeing only this problem, that difficulty. We can get overtaken by a heavy, dark feeling of despair. But when we experience a sense of gratitude, we give ourselves a dose of mental sunshine. Suddenly the world seems brighter, and we have more options.

And the greatest thing is that as we experience the mental sunshine of gratitude, we begin to glow with sunshine ourselves. Suddenly not only is the world brighter, but we are too. Soon we notice that our lives are full of people who want to be around us because we exude peacefulness, happiness, and joy.

Gratitude Promotes Health

Feelings of gratitude release positive endorphins throughout the body, creating health.

—SHARON HUFFMAN

Josephine is a seventy-seven-year-old woman who, in her late fifties, was diagnosed with a malignant brain tumor and scheduled for surgery a few days later. While waiting for the operation, she sat in her porch swing and gave thanks for all the wonderful things in her life. She wrote a letter of thanks to each of her family members, called them around her, and went into the hospital. The night before surgery, she suddenly saw "what looked like a beautiful woman with long, flowing hair smiling at me and radiating light. She said she was an angel who felt my love and she had come to reassure me that everything was OK; that I would have plenty of time to fulfill my life's purpose. And then she said, 'Always remember that it was your love and your appreciation that brought healing to you.' " It turned out that the tumor was gone, and Josephine was sent home without surgery.

Not all healings are as miraculous as Josephine's, but recent scientific research has begun to indicate that positive emotions, such as gratitude and love, have beneficial effects on health. They do so by strengthening and enhancing the immune system, which enables the body to resist disease and recover more quickly from illness, through the release of endorphins into the bloodstream. Endorphins are the body's natural painkillers. Among other effects, they stimulate dilation of the blood vessels, which leads to a relaxed heart.

Conversely, negative emotions such as worry, anger, and hopelessness reduce the number and slow down the movement of disease-fighting white cells in our bloodstreams, and contribute to the development of stroke and heart disease by dumping high levels of adrenaline into the bloodstream. Adrenaline constricts blood vessels, particularly to the heart, raising blood pressure and potentially damaging arteries and the heart itself.

What this means is that the more we experience a sense of gratitude, the more endorphins and the less adrenaline we pump into our systems, thus contributing to longer, healthier lives. As we count our blessings, we literally bathe ourselves inwardly in good hormones. And while we can't guarantee that a sense of appreciation will cure us as it did Josephine, we can be sure that it will make us feel better!

Gratitude Eradicates Worry

You cannot be grateful and unhappy at the same time.

—A WOMAN TO DR. TOM COSTA

If worrying were a paying job, I would be a rich woman. Somehow during my childhood, I got the idea that worrying could actually stave off future disaster, and as I entered adulthood, I became convinced that if I were to stop worrying, took my eye off the ball, as it were, that something dreadful would happen. If I worried enough about being poor, I wouldn't be. If I worried enough about my partner's safety, nothing would happen to him. If I worried enough about my stepson's health, he wouldn't get sick. There was no room in my heart for happiness because worry took up all the space. (Indeed I was convinced that if I were too happy, it would somehow hex the situation. If I got too happy about love, for example, I wouldn't worry sufficiently and therefore it would be taken from me.)

In my forties, I have been working on letting go of my compulsive worrying, and I have been amazed at how swiftly a sense of gratefulness banishes the worry warts. And I've tried many other things—asking myself what is the worst thing that could happen and imagining going through that to a new place; noticing without judgment my worry; indulging it; pushing it away. None of these has been as effective as tapping into a sense of appreciation in this moment for what I do have.

Worried about money? I focus on the fact that so far, I have always had what I needed and right now, I have enough. Worried about health? I focus on the amount of good health I'm thankful to be experiencing right now. Worried about—my favorite—a loved one being taken suddenly in an accident? I focus on how grateful I am that they are in my life right now.

I think tapping into the wellspring of gratitude works for two reasons. First, worry is always about the future, if only the next hour or minute, whereas gratitude is in the here and now. Cast over your list of worries. Aren't they always about what might or might not happen? You are worried about the reaction of your boss tomorrow to your presentation. You're worried about how you are going to afford to send your son to college. You're worried about the test results. In every case, you project yourself into the future and imagine something bad happening. As André Dubus points out, "It is not hard to live through a day if you can live through a moment. What creates despair is the imagination, which pretends there is a future and insists on predicting millions of moments, thousands of days, and so drains you that you cannot live the moment at hand."

THE GIFTS OF GRATITUDE

Gratitude brings you back to the present moment, to all that is working perfectly right now. Tomorrow may bring difficulties, but for right now, things are pretty good.

Gratefulness also eliminates worry because it reminds us of the abundance of our universe. Yes, something bad might happen, but given all that you have received so far, chances are you will continue to be supported on your journey through life, even in ways you would never have guessed or chosen for yourself.

Gratitude Draws People to Us

Sometimes I go about with pity for
myself and all the while Great Winds
are carrying me across the sky.

—OJIBWAY SAYING

I have a friend who can't seem to find one good thing about her life. She complains constantly about her job, her coworkers, and her relationships with men. She puts herself down a good bit, too. It does

no good whatsoever for me to point out all the good things that I see in her life. It just starts another round of "poor me." After I spend an afternoon with her, I feel cranky, depressed, and, frankly, bored. I notice that I try to avoid getting together with her.

The opposite is true about my friend Abby. Abby has had a hard life, too. She wasn't born into a wealthy family; she has raised a son by herself, put herself through college, and taken care of aged and ill relatives. But she is cheerful and upbeat most of the time, and I love being around her, because when we're together, life seems easy and joyful.

Recently, I made the observation that she had a great career and seemed to be appreciated by her boss and company. She replied, "Oh, yes! I love my job and I'm lucky to have it. Every morning when I drive to work, I grab the steering wheel and thank God for my job. For the job that paid for this nice car I wouldn't have otherwise, for the nice people I work with in a beautiful office and for a boss that treats me and everyone else so well. I'm absolutely grateful for what I have and make a point to give thanks on my way to work. It grounds me and starts off my day on a positive note."

I am convinced that it is Abby's sense of gratitude that gives her such an upbeat attitude. It's also why she has more friends than anyone I know. For when we are grateful, we exude happiness and that makes us magnets that draw people toward us. They want to be around that exuberant energy.

Gratitude not only draws people to us, but it helps us keep those who are in our sphere. When we see the glass as half-full, rather than half-empty, we notice what is there rather than dwelling on what is not. When we notice what's there, we get out of our self-absorption and realize that there are people around us, many of whom have done wonderful things for us. And when we express our gratitude for their presence in our lives, it's more likely that those people will want to continue to be around us.

Gratitude Is the Antidote to Bitterness and Resentment

The more light you allow within you, the brighter the world you live in will be.

—SHAKTI GAWAIN

Twenty years ago, Cynthia, a petite, talented woman in her late twenties, got divorced in a terrible breakup. Two decades later, bitter and resentful, she is still obsessed with her ex-husband, bad-mouthing him to her children and friends whenever she gets a chance, convinced that he ruined her life. In a way, of course, he did. Because she kept focusing on her pain and resentment, she was never able to heal and move on. Hurt and hateful, she hasn't been able to attract new love in her life, and her now-grown children avoid her like the plague.

Have you ever met someone so bitter about their life that they feel like a black hole sucking away all the energy around them? Whether we call them pessimists, ingrates, or those who always see the glass as half-empty, they are a drag to be around. So focused on what hasn't worked for them they can't see the ways they have been the recipients of gifts, blessings, and surprises.

Most of us aren't total black holes, but when we fail to give thanks for what happens in our lives, we can get hung up in bitterness that prevents us from developing emotionally and spiritually. If we fail to grow, the light inside us grows dim.

THE GIFTS OF GRATITUDE

Bitterness is a poison that snuffs the light of our souls, hardening us to life's pleasures and joys by keeping us focused only on what is wrong. When the man I lived with for fourteen years left me, he said it was because I was turning bitter and he didn't want to stick around to see it. Although there were other reasons for our breakup, including many he was responsible for, after the pain of the loss had subsided I gave thanks to him for the wake-up call; I was turning into a resentful woman, and that was the last thing on Earth I wanted to be.

I'm determined not to sink into bitterness again. While there are plenty of things in life to be justifiably annoyed, angry, or hurt at, that doesn't mean that I should completely ignore all that is beautiful, good, and touching. I want my soul to shine with an overflowing of love, and practicing gratitude is one of the best ways I know to do it.

Gratitude is a inner light that we can use to illumine our souls. The more we are thankful, the more light we experience and the more we shine forth into the world.

Gratitude Cures Perfectionism

A point worth pondering: Upon complet-
ing the Universe, the Great Creator pro-
nounced it "very good." Not "perfect."

—SARAH BAN BREATHNACH

When I was young, I wanted to be a saint. Not just
plain old good, but a bona fide canonized saint.
I figured that anything worth doing was worth
doing perfectly, and while I was being perfect, I
might as well get all the adoration that perfectionism deserves. Sainthood seemed to fit the bill.
Unfortunately, I kept slipping up: I would forget to
make my bed or get jealous of my little brother, and
then sink into despair, convinced I was a complete
failure.

Ah, perfectionism! Those of us afflicted with
the pesky bug may look with amazement (You
mean you don't care you didn't do it perfectly??) or
disdain (What kind of lazy, good-for-nothing guy
are you?) upon those who don't suffer from it, but
the truth, of course, is that it springs from our own
sense of lack. We simply don't believe we're good

enough as we are in our humble, human, imperfect state, and must therefore compensate by being Miss Perfect Goody-Two-Shoes.

That was certainly true for me. Somehow, as a child, I got the message that if only I did everything perfectly, life would be OK. But life has a way of being messy and imperfectable, despite our best efforts, and individuals, including myself, are equally incapable of perfection. After decades of being a wannabe saint, I finally got worn out from trying. Now, instead of attempting to make everyone and everything fit my plan (an impossible task, even for a saint), I spend the energy I used to pour into sainthood school to be more grateful.

Because perfectionism is born of a sense of inadequacy, of lack, an attitude of gratitude counteracts it by tapping us into the experience of abundance. Gratitude makes our world feel complete and right. When we feel the fullness of gratitude, we accept life just as it is—however messy, complicated, and drawn-outside-the-lines that may be.

Gratitude not only helps us accept that the world is imperfect, but that we are too—and that's OK. For when we pour the oil of appreciation for life in all its imperfections over our experience, we ourselves can't help but be anointed. Suddenly seized by joy for the crazy, mixed-up world, we recognize ourselves as part of that world, and take our rightful place as a child of the Universe, perfectly acceptable in all our imperfection.

Gratitude Releases Us from the "Gimmes"

If there is to be any peace it will come through being, not having.

—HENRY MILLER

A few years ago, I noticed that if a weekend went by without my buying something other than food for the week, I got an itchy feeling. I wanted to shop, to buy, to consume—it didn't matter what. I didn't actually need anything, but I wanted to purchase something.

I don't think I was alone in the feeling. Consumer debt is at the highest level in U.S. history, as are personal bankruptcies. We're literally buying ourselves into financial holes too large for many of us to crawl out of.

I didn't like feeling that I was a slave to shopping. So I decided to buy less and appreciate what I already had more. Instead of a new blouse, I wore an old favorite. But instead of just putting it on mindlessly, I tried really noticing what I liked about it: the delicate embroidery, the silky feel of the satin, the vibrant shade of red. That's when I discovered one of the greatest gifts of gratitude—it gets us off the consuming treadmill so many of us are caught on. Here's how.

A perennial dieting tip is to eat something and then wait twenty minutes before deciding to eat something again. The reason is that your body needs that much time to register that it is full. If you keep eating without pausing, you will not realize that your body is full, and therefore you may overeat.

Giving thanks for what we have in our lives is like that pause when eating. It allows us to feel full, to register on the emotional and spiritual level that we have, in fact, been given "enough." If we don't practice gratitude on a daily basis, it's easy to overconsume, to feel a lack and to try to fill that lack through possessions, because on a psychological level we haven't registered that we already have what we need.

I've spent years talking about this to people, but the only way to really get it is to try it yourself. For two weeks, don't buy anything new except food. Try really to take in the gifts you already have, not just the wonderful intangible ones such as good health or love in your life, but the material ones as well— your cozy apartment, the green pitcher your mother gave you, the gargoyle bookends, your favorite earrings. Walk around where you live and really notice and give thanks for the objects in your life that give you joy. Then notice what effect it has on your desire to buy more.

Gratitude Keeps Us Current

That it will never come again is
what makes life so sweet.

—EMILY DICKINSON

Last night I watched my daughter Ana, whom we recently adopted from China, lie on the bed in an ecstatic trance of bottle-sucking. Her eyes closed, her rosebud mouth pursed, her exquisitely long fingers curled around the plastic bottle, she gave herself over to the experience. She wasn't obsessing on past wounds, although perhaps she had a right to. Neglected for over a year, when we got her she had second-degree burns on her buttocks from lying in urine. Nor was she worrying about where future bottles might come from, although she had a right to do that also. Abandoned on Christmas evening on a cold street until someone heard her newborn cries, she had been fed only watered-down milk and seemed to be starving the first few weeks we fed her.

Rather, she was so focused on appreciating the warm milk as it went down her throat that everything else, past and future, simply disappeared. As I looked at her, I realized that this total and complete absorption in the present moment is available to us all when we choose to let gratitude wash over us uninhibitedly.

But many of us have been taught not to give ourselves over so fully to something or someone.

ATTITUDES OF GRATITUDE

As a child, I believed that you couldn't let yourself become totally immersed in an experience, because something bad might be happening as your attention is diverted. My parents used to say that as a child they never saw me asleep; I always had one eye open, alert to disaster.

But if Ana, who has suffered so much in her very short life, can give herself over to the joy of completely appreciating her bottle, can't I allow myself in this moment to fully appreciate the sweet peas on my desk, the wonder of being able to think and read and write?

As I allow myself to open to the fullness of gratitude, the past and future fade away and I become more alive in the present moment. That's because gratitude is, for the most part, about the here and now. While we can be thankful for past blessings and hope for future ones, when we experience a sense of gratefulness, we are usually contemplating some present circumstance. We are brought up to date with ourselves. Our focus moves away from all that we or others did or failed to do in the past, or what we hope for or worry about in the future, and we find ourselves placed squarely in this precious moment, this experience that will never happen again.

Gratitude Opens Our Hearts

*The most invisible creators I know of are
those artists whose medium is life itself.
The ones who express the inexpress-
ible—without brush, hammer, clay or
guitar. They neither paint nor sculpt—
their medium is their being. Whatever
their presence touches has increased
life. They see and don't have to draw.
They are the artists of being alive.*

—J. STONE

I spent several Christmases recently with a family that loves to give presents. Every year, the floor
around the tree was heaped with hundreds of gifts,
so many that it took the entire morning to open
them all. But despite all that was given and received,
I would leave there every year feeling empty and
alone. There had been a plethora of presents, but

no presence. This family gave so many gifts because they didn't know how to connect deeply to themselves and one another. They ripped through the mounds of merchandise, saying a pro forma "Thank you," but no sense of true appreciation was expressed or received.

The experience was so powerful—the contrast between the material plenty and the emotional lack—it set me to thinking. That's when I realized that you can't experience gratitude with a closed heart. It's just not possible. Gratefulness is only experienced in the moments in which we open our hearts to life—to the beauty in this moment, to the possibility of surprise in the next.

A person does something kind for you, even a very small thing, say, holding a door open for you. When you say, "Thank you" and really mean it, rather than saying it out of social convention, your heart instinctively opens to the person. In that moment, you experience your connection to one another, even if you never lay eyes on each other again.

Openheartedness takes courage. It requires enough trust in the goodness of other people and the universe at large that we can put aside our self-protectiveness—that stance that says I am not going to be grateful for what I am receiving right now because it's too scary to risk getting hurt—and take a leap of faith to acknowledge that we have received a gift.

The fact that true gratitude creates a sense of openheartedness is the reason so much of the "thanks" in this culture is rote and unfeeling. People are afraid to feel thankful, because they are afraid of the out-of-control experience that occurs when they acknowledge the bond between giver and receiver. We are afraid to feel the love that gets created any time we express true thanks. As adults, our hearts have been broken many times and, by golly, we want to make sure it doesn't happen again.

The choice is ours, in every moment. Do we want to live in seeming safety, shut inside the shell of our individuality, unwilling to experience the deep and abiding connections that are ours in any case, or are we willing to risk, over and over, having our hearts broken open to the beauty and the pain of all that is ours to experience?

When do you experience an open heart? What are the conditions that foster your willingness to open your heart? As we practice true gratitude, we learn to take the risk over and over again.

Gratitude Spawns Kindness and Generosity

Our work-a-day lives are filled with opportunities to bless others. The power of a single glance or an encouraging smile must never be underestimated.

—G. RICHARD RIEGER

Deborah Chamberin-Taylor had been studying Buddhism in Thailand, at a monastery where all the teaching, housing, and meals were free. Shortly before she left, a Thai family came and made a meal for the 250 retreatants as a way of expressing their gratitude for the teachings of the Buddha.

Shortly thereafter, Deborah was helping to plan a weekend retreat in Northern California. The planning group was discussing how to feed lunch to all

THE GIFTS OF GRATITUDE

those who would be attending, because the cost of the meal was not in the budget. Filled with a sense of gratitude for the generosity of the Thai family, Deborah found herself volunteering to pay for lunch for all the participants. "I noticed what joy it brought me to consider giving such a gift. . . . Later, when I told this story to a group, I was pleasantly surprised when person after person walked up and handed me unsolicited money for the 'lunch fund.' They also wanted to be part of fueling the 'cycle of generosity.' "

As Deborah's story shows, gratitude begets generosity which begets gratitude which begets generosity. Gratitude creates a sense of fullness. And from this fullness, we feel moved to give. That's because true kindness and generosity come from a response to this fullness: we give best from overflow.

It's a beautiful cycle. The more you feel grateful, the stronger is the impulse toward giving. And the more you give, the more you get—love, friendship, a sense of purpose and accomplishment, even, some-times, material wealth. As author Lewis Smedes notes, "When I feel the joy of receiving a gift my heart nudges me to join creation's ballet, the airy dance of giving and receiving, and getting and giving again."

It doesn't have to be an extravagant, expensive gift. When we live with a grateful heart, we will see endless opportunities to give: a flower from the garden to a coworker, a kind word to our child, a visit to an old person. You will know what to do.

Gratitude Joins Us to All Life

I feel this communion, this strange attunement, most readily with large white pines, a little less with sugar maples, beeches, or oaks. Clearly white pines and I are on the same wave-length. What I give back to the trees I cannot imagine. I hope they receive something, because trees are among my closest friends.

—ANNE LABASTILLE

In *The Continuum Concept*, Jean Liedloff describes a profound experience she had when she was eight years old of the connection that Anne Labastille describes. "The incident happened during a nature walk in the Maine woods where I was at summer camp. I was last in line; I had fallen back a bit and was hurrying to catch up when, through the trees, I saw a glade. It had a lush fir tree at the far side and a knoll in the center covered in bright, almost luminous green moss. The rays of the afternoon sun slanted against the blue-black green of the pine forest. The little roof of visible sky was perfectly blue. The whole picture had a completeness, an all-there quality of such dense power that it stopped me in my tracks.... Everything was in its place—the tree, the earth underneath, the rock, the moss. In autumn it would be right; in winter under the snow, it would be perfect in its wintriness. Spring would come again and miracle within miracle would unfold, each at its special pace, some things having died off, some sprouting in their first spring, but all of equal and utter rightness....

"That night in my camp bed I brought The Glade to mind and was filled with a sense of thankfulness, and renewed my vow to preserve my vision."

"With every leaf a miracle ..." writes Walt Whitman in his poetic tribute to lilacs, and this is

what he is talking about—when we are in touch with a profound sense of gratitude, we connect to all of life, recognizing the miracle in the tallest tree, the smallest bug.

Such a sense of connection is purely joyful; it grants to our human endeavors no more or less importance than they should have, and inspires us to do whatever we can to conserve and protect all of the natural wonders of the Earth and sea, not just those that are convenient for us. Thus gratitude also gives birth to a fiercely loving environmentalism, a sensitivity born of the connection made explicit between us and everything else that creeps, crawls, sways, and clings. We recognize that we cannot live outside of the great web of life that lovingly holds us in its nurturing embrace, and we vow to protect the sanctity of that web.

Gratitude Connects Us to Spirit

If the only prayer you say in your whole life is "thank you," that would suffice.

—MEISTER ECKHART

Marjory is a former "jeweler to the stars" who made one-of-a-kind rings and other extraordinary pieces for such luminaries as Tina Turner. Her business boomed and the good times did indeed roll. When gold prices skyrocketed, however, her business went bust and she became a recluse in a small cabin. But she refused to feel sorry for herself.

On a flight during a recent job-hunting trip, Marjory was seated by Paul, a charming and sweet Baptist teenager from South Carolina on his way to China. Now, it's easy to figure out within a couple of minutes of meeting Marjory that her religious leanings are fairly New Age, especially as she goes over her complete astrological chart with you right off the bat! In any case, the two were chatting away when Marjory noticed the spectacular sunset diffusing golden and fuchsia light, turning the Pacific Ocean into a pool of amber glass. "Oh, God. Look at that. How beautiful!" Marjory exclaimed, her eyes tearing over.

Paul turned to Marjory gravely and asked, "Who is your God?"

Taken aback, Marjory replied that her God was just God and she didn't worry much about where

ATTITUDES OF GRATITUDE

he came from. The teen pressed to know if her God was the Father of his personal Savior, Jesus Christ. Marjory stared back, glassy-eyed, when a small miracle took place.

Paul began quoting from Psalm 23, a magnificent and lyrical stream of biblical poetry about how beautiful this home is that God had made for us. Marjory and everyone else within earshot relaxed instantly and looked at the sunset, seeing again, through the eyes of timeless wonder and gratitude, the marvel of this world we live in.

However you experience God—as loving Father, nurturing Mother, Creator of all that is, your Higher Power, the Spirit of Kindness and Compassion, whatever is true for you—the quickest, easiest way to connect to Him/Her/It is to express your gratitude. That's because gratitude is the response to the giver of a gift—and when we give thanks for things beyond the gifts we receive from other people, we are de facto thanking the Greater Power for what we have received: food, shelter, the beautiful sunny day, life itself. As we give thanks, our spirits join with the Great Spirit in the dance of life that is the interplay between giver and receiver.

I love the sensibility of this exchange that is inherent in Native American spirituality. Whenever a person is about to take the life of something—a deer, a tree—he or she humbly asks permission of the Spirit that dwells in the animal or plant, and gives thanks for their willingness to sacrifice their own life. Sometimes, an offering, such as a pinch of corn or tobacco, is given in compensation. Such an act acknowledges that something has been given and received on both sides.

Gratitude Opens Us to Moments of Grace

Nobody can conceive or imagine all the wonders there are unseen and unsee-able in the world.

—FRANCIS P. CHURCH

Morihei Ueshiba, the father of Aikido, once described an experience he had walking alone in his garden. Suddenly "I felt that a golden spirit sprang up from the ground. . . . My mind and body turned into light.

I was able to understand the whispering of the birds, and was clearly aware of the mind of God ... the spirit of loving protection for all beings. Endless tears of joy streamed down my cheeks. Since that time, I have grown to feel that the whole earth is my house...."

Have you ever had an experience in which you slip out of ordinary space and time and tap into the flow of the universe, where there is no separation between you and everything else and where everything seems perfectly right just as it is? Some people find such moments of transcendence through meditation, others in nature, still others when making love. As a young child, I often experienced such moments in the early spring tromping alone in the icy stream near my house.

Such moments are rare gifts, in which we open to an expansive, ecstatic state of Big Mind, the place where all is right with us and the world. These moments of grace are so rare and so wonderful that many spiritual seekers spend a lifetime trying to experience them. And the desire to feel such expansiveness is often the impetus for taking mind-altering drugs.

I'm convinced that you don't have to meditate for years on a mountaintop or take LSD to experience such transcendence. All you have to do is tap into the fullness of a sense of gratitude, and grace will likely descend. (Indeed, I am sure that what meditation and mind-altering drugs do is break down the barriers to experiencing gratitude in its full abundance.)

We can't force or demand such magical mystical experiences. But we can offer ourselves up as willing and worthy participants by reveling in the wonders that we are already experiencing. Through gratitude, our souls, in Emily Dickinson's words, "always stand ajar; ready to welcome the ecstatic experience."

CHAPTER 3

The Attitudes of Gratitude

The most powerful agent of growth and transformation is something much more basic than any technique: a change of heart.

—JOHN WELWOOD

The next step on the journey is to look at the attitudes of gratitude—those beliefs that foster a sense of thankfulness. Attitudes are the underpinnings of action; as John Welwood implies, we can't change on the outside until and unless we transform our thinking, transform the way we imagine ourselves and our reality. The good news is that we really can decide to see the glass as half-full rather than half-empty, and that decision will have profoundly positive effects not only on our happiness and that of those around us, but on the way our whole lives unfold.

Life Is a Miracle

The Zen master Ling Chi said that the miracle is not to walk on burning charcoal or in the thin air or on the water; the miracle is just to walk on earth. You breathe in. You become aware of the fact that you are alive. You are still alive and you are walking on this beautiful planet.... The greatest of all miracles is to be alive.

—THICH NHAT HANH

Thich Nhat Hanh is a Vietnamese Buddhist monk who now lives in exile in France. While living in Vietnam, he endured all kinds of hardships, including the killings by either the French, American, or Vietnamese military of family members and friends. An orphanage that he started was bombed. And yet he is a walking example of joy and gratitude. When asked how he survived such difficulties with such peace and love in his heart, he replied that every morning he used to ask himself what he could count on that day; sometimes it was only the blue sky and the brown earth, and the fact that he was still breathing in and out. But in counting his blessings, so to speak, he reconnected to the miracle that he was, at least for the present moment, still alive in this beautiful world. "Suffering is not enough. Life is both dreadful and wonderful," he reminds us. "How can I smile when I am filled with so much sorrow? It is natural—you need to smile to your sorrow because you are more than your sorrow."

Buddhist and Sufi teachers spend a lot of time talking about "waking up," by which they mean, I think, living life to its fullest because we are aware of living it moment to moment. Aware of breathing in, aware of breathing out; aware of chewing and swallowing our food; aware of placing one foot in front of the other when walking. Aware of seeing your infant son, of the effect of your words on a coworker, of the fact that your one foot is resting on top of the other.

Spiritual leaders teach that waking up is a process, that it doesn't just happen once and for all, but must occur again and again when we realize we have forgotten the miracle of being alive, and in recognizing our forgetfulness, we wake to the miracle once again. In the moments we are awake to the wonder of simply being alive, gratitude flows, no matter our circumstances.

When times have been tough for me, I have done a similar practice to Thich Nhat Hanh's. Before getting up in the morning, I have asked myself what I could count on that day, both externally—that I still had a place to live and food on the table; and internally—the deep love and trust, for example, that I feel for my friends.

It's a wonderful antidote to worry and opens you to gratitude, provided that you really stick to what you can count on today. Sometimes I would find

myself, for instance, when I thought about the fact
that I had a house, saying, "Yes, but I don't know if
I can afford it tomorrow and what if the earthquake
strikes, and . . . ." Then I would choose to stop and
say, "This is just for today. What can you count on
today?" As we learn how to appreciate the miracle
of being alive, we will find the peace and the
strength to face life's challenges as they come.

The Universe Is Friendly

*Einstein was asked what he thought the
most important question was that a
human being needed to answer. His reply
was "Is the universe friendly or not?"*

—JOAN BORYSENKO

For most of my life, I have subscribed to the "Watch
out—disaster might strike at any time, so don't get
too complacent" school. It probably comes as no
surprise that I have suffered from chronic muscle
spasms in my back and neck my whole life; even
my body is perpetually tensed for trouble. By age

forty-four, I was just plain sick of it, tired of waiting for the boom to fall, tired of clenching in fear rather than opening in expectation. So I decided to live as if the universe were friendly.

I have been meditating on Einstein's question for over a year now, and I am convinced that how each of us answers it is the key to whether we are happy and joy-filled or not, and whether or not an attitude of gratitude comes easily. If we believe the universe is friendly, then we believe that life is on our side, that good things will come our way, and that even when bad things happen, they are bumps in the road designed to teach us to become more wise, more whole, more loving. In this view of the universe, gratitude flows from us naturally, as an instinctive response to the bounty we perceive all around us.

If, on the other hand, we believe the universe is unfriendly, then we see our life as an endless struggle against difficult odds, we believe that bad things are either random or sent purposely to torture us, that there is nothing we can count on and therefore we must brace ourselves for the next crisis, hoarding what we have. In this view, gratitude is very situation-specific. We're grateful—maybe—when things go well, but we are always ready for the boom to fall and for it all to disappear.

I have lapses in believing in the friendly universe, particularly when things are going badly money-wise. When I forget, I take out a piece of paper on which I've copied down a piece of an Inuit teaching: "The inhabitant or soul of the universe is never seen; its voice alone is heard. All we know is that it has a gentle voice, like a woman a voice so fine . . . that even children cannot become afraid. And what it says is 'Sila ersinarsinivdluge,' 'Be not afraid of the universe.'" It helps me remember that if I place my trust in the beneficence of the universe, things tend to work out. And if they don't, at least in the meantime I will enjoy myself a whole lot more and be more fun to be around.

Let Gratitude Flow Naturally

One's destination is never a place but rather a new way of looking at things.

—HENRY MILLER

Nothing destroys a sense of gratitude faster than being told we "should" feel grateful. Some "should"s are necessary, e.g. in teaching manners to children (children learn not only by example, but by pairing instruction to example). But when we try to experience gratitude as a living force in our lives, guilt, whether imposed by others or by ourselves, is deadly.

We've probably all had someone in our lives tell us we should be grateful for something, or perhaps we say it to ourselves. Either way, this is the least likely way to promote an attitude of gratitude. As far as I can tell, gratitude is generated in two ways: one, by a spontaneous upswelling of the heart toward the wonder of life and all its particulars; and two, by a conscious decision to practice looking at what's right in our lives rather than focusing on what's missing. Either way, we don't get to gratitude by guilt-trips.

Guilt is a terrible motivator. It makes us want to run away from whatever is making us feel bad, and to avoid looking at whatever is underlying it.

I say this because I don't want you, after reading this book, to go away thinking you "should" feel grateful. I want to encourage us all to open our hearts and experience gratitude as much as we can. But I know for myself that there are days when it is impossible for me to feel thankful for anything no matter how hard I try—and if that's true for you sometimes, be gentle with yourself. The more you allow what is true for you to be true, and the less you "should" yourself, the more space you create for the possibility of gratitude to quietly, softly enter your heart.

The Flashlight in Your Own Backyard

Inside yourself or outside, you never have to change what you see, only the way you see it.

—THADDEUS GOLAS

I went to see my father in the hospital about a week before he died. He had suffered for years with emphysema, hooked up to an oxygen tank, barely able to move around, and was failing fast. Bedridden, he was on constant oxygen and medication; his six-foot-two frame weighed only 130 pounds because eating anything but ice cream was too difficult. Every breath was a labored struggle. I asked him whether the quality of his life was worth all the effort. "I still enjoy being alive," he responded. "Sometimes it's easier to breathe and then I really enjoy just quietly taking a breath. I still enjoy reading the comics in the newspaper and watching the ball games on TV. My life is good." He said not a word about all that he had lost, all that he would never do again.

When I was about to do publicity for *A Grateful Heart*, I talked to my friend Dawna Markova about how to speak about the power of gratitude. She's great at metaphors, which are wonderful ways to look at things from a new perspective. What she said I have carried with me ever since: "Gratitude is like a flashlight. If you go out in your yard at night and turn on a flashlight, you suddenly can see what's there. It was always there, but you couldn't see it in the dark."

Exactly! Gratitude lights up what is already there. You don't necessarily have anything more or

different, but suddenly you can actually see what is. And because you can see, you no longer take it for granted. You're just standing in your yard, but suddenly you realize, Oh, there's the first flower of spring struggling to emerge from the snow; Oh, there's a deer emerging from the scrub brush; Oh, there's the measuring cup you've been looking for that your daughter was using to make mud pies. It's just your ordinary old backyard, but suddenly you are filled with happiness, thankfulness, and joy.

That's what my father did. Shining the light of gratitude on his life, he saw what was there that was good.

The great thing about the flashlight of gratitude is that you can use it day or night, no matter where you are or what your circumstances. It works whether we are young or old, fat or thin, rich or poor, sick or well. All we need to do is turn it on.

What it takes to turn it on varies from person to person. There was a renowned surgeon at a week-long workshop who, when asked what surprised or inspired him that week, said, "Nothing." He was invested in being cynical. But something disturbed him; he knew he had "flunked" the test the workshop leader presented—and he was the kind of guy who always ended up at the head of the class. So he began to look around for things to report to the leader. By week's end, he was genuinely engaged in the excitement and wonder of life again. Even the other workshop participants noticed the difference.

It's All Gratuitous

This is what binds all people and all creation together—the gratuity of the gift of being.

—MATTHEW FOX

"My only son died five years ago; he was four and a half," writes a contributor to *Slowing Down in a Speeded Up World.* "One of the gifts his death brought was an excuse to stop the rush. For the first year, I allowed grief to wash over me whenever I needed to, and I let myself be open to the healing that surrounds us in this incredible world. I had time for a hug and to talk with my friends; I had vast amounts of time to cherish four and a half years of memories.

"Nowadays it isn't unusual for me to stop in my tracks when a rainbow arches over the bay outside my office window, or a tiny feather drifts down to me from the sky, or a child's laugh at McDonald's brings tears to my eyes.

"I realize how lucky I am, not to have lost my son but to have had him for as long as I did. I'm lucky to have known the importance of certain moments that catch your soul and may never come again."

Gratefulness, or "great fullness" as Brother David Steindl-Rast calls it, "is the full response of the human heart to the gratuitousness of all that is." He and Matthew Fox remind us that truly every single thing we have has been given to us, not necessarily because we deserve it, but gratuitously, for no known reason, and that the same is true for every living thing. We are connected one to another, to sky and water and tree and snake, by virtue of being here together as part of the wheel of life. Whatever source we believe is the giver—some concept of God or the randomness of the Big Bang— the fact of our incarnation, the fact of the lizard's skin, the rose's scent, the blueness of the sky, is an incredible gift. None of us—bee, flower, person—did anything to earn this gift, nor is anything required of us in return.

When, in a sudden moment—gazing at a field of daffodils, perhaps, or moving luxuriously through warm water, or listening to the painfully beautiful voice of Billie Holiday—we are struck by the truth of this amazingly free "no strings attached" gift, gratitude flows naturally from us, without effort. At such times, we don't need to work at feeling thankful; we just are.

In such transcendent moments, we take our place in the great wheel of life, recognizing our connection to one another and to all of creation. More than that, we actually become part of everything, so that we experience the truth that there is no separation between us and everything else, sound, sight, and feeling.

At such times, gratitude opens our hearts fully and we take in the love, the beauty, the joy that is ours to possess in every moment, in all circumstances. Through the gift of a grateful heart, we merge with the All and remember our rightful home.

A Habit of the Heart

In relation to others, gratitude is good
manners; in relation to ourselves,
it is a habit of the heart and a spiritual
discipline.

—DAPHNE ROSE KINGMA

As a young woman in my twenties and thirties,
I learned a great deal about thankfulness from
Daphne Rose Kingma. We spent a lot of time together
working on books, and again and again I would
watch her make a personal connection to the people
who came across her path—garbage collectors,
long-distance operators, or the person selling coffee
on the corner. No matter what was going on in
her own life, no matter how rushed or upset she
was, she took the time to connect. I'd hear her on
the phone with the airline reservations desk. In the
course of getting a flight she'd learn the woman's
name, where she lived, and the fact that she, like
Daphne, loved flashy high heels. Daphne was so
genuinely appreciative of the other person's help
that the person on the other end of the phone felt

washed in a warm bath of love. It was then I realized that while gratitude was a feeling, it could be cultivated. I set out to emulate her (although I still am not as good at it as she).

One of the fascinating things about feelings is that they come and go, like waves in the ocean of our consciousness. Happiness, anger, fear, love, thankfulness—they arise in response to some external or internal trigger and then subside. We feel angry, and then we don't. We are "in love" and then we aren't. We feel thankful, and then it's over. It's particularly easy to see the tide of feelings in a child, where they come and go so quickly and uncensoredly. One minute my daughter is screaming her head off because I have left the room; I return and pick her up—a big smile.

As we grow, one of our spiritual tasks is to move beyond this purely emotional response to life and begin to cultivate positive emotions as "habits of the heart," as Daphne calls them. What this means is that we learn to love even when we don't "feel" loving, be kind when we'd rather be surly, and feel grateful when we don't particularly feel like being thankful. In this way, we turn feelings, which come and go, into conscious attitudes that we act upon even if we don't "feel" like it.

Our attitudes are our mental stances, the positions we hold vis-à-vis life. In some ways, our attitudes determine everything, because they are the glasses through which we see the world. Is the world a wonderful place or a hellhole? All of us know that the answer to that question depends on our attitude on any given day. Has the world changed? Most likely our thinking about it has. When we consciously cultivate positive attitudes, such as love, joy, and gratitude, we begin to "remake" the world. We literally live in a different place because our attitudes about it have changed.

The particular beauty of an attitude of gratitude is that it instantly connects us to everything else. In an important way, it is the recognition of the connection, the switch, between us and the rest of life. And consciously recognizing it opens the flow: the more grateful we are, the more of an abundant sense of life we will experience.

For that's the irony about the relationship between attitudes and feelings. The more you cultivate the attitude, even if you don't feel it, the more you experience the feeling. The more loving we are, the more love we feel. The more joy we radiate, the more comes back our way. And the more thankful we are, the more we experience the richness of spirit that grateful feelings produce.

Attitude Is the Only Disability

We who lived in concentration camps can remember the men who walked through the huts comforting others, giving away their last piece of bread. They may have been few in number, but they offer sufficient proof that everything can be taken from a man but one thing: the last of the human freedoms—to choose one's attitude in any given set of circumstances. . . .

—VICTOR FRANKL

My friend Annette needs a kidney transplant. Everyone who knows her is amazed at her grateful attitude. Upon hearing the news, rather than adopting

a "poor me" stance, she focused on the fact that while waiting for the transplant, she qualifies for a less invasive dialysis method. In telling me about the situation she proclaimed with a radiant face, "I am so thankful. I have four people who have volunteered to be tested to see if they can be a donor. Isn't that great! Four people are willing to give me a kidney."

I thought of Annette as I was driving the other day and saw a bumper sticker that proclaimed, "Attitude Is the Only Disability." While I am sure it was a slogan for disabled people's rights, I suddenly realized its larger implications—what we think about our lives, our attitude—has the ability to enable or disable us. As many spiritual teachers have said, we cannot necessarily change our circumstances. But we have complete control over what we think about our circumstances, the meaning we attach to them. No matter our circumstances —even, as Victor Frankl points out, in a situation as horrifying as a concentration camp—we can focus on the positive and make a difference by virtue of our attitude.

Because of her attitude of gratitude, Annette may be "sick," but she is not dis-abled. Through gratitude, she is enhancing her ability to renew and re-create, which comes, as Joan Borysenko puts it, "when we lift ourselves out of the familiar axis and see life from a higher perspective." She is attracting all kinds of people who want to help, everyone from kidney donors and energy healers to coworkers offering to give her their comp time and folks volunteering to cook and clean for her while she's recuperating. We all want to be around her because she is such a teacher of gratitude and joyfulness.

Like no one else, she has proven to me that gratitude is an attitude that can be consciously chosen, no matter what our circumstances. We can focus on the negative and descend into a spiral of negativity and gloom. Or we can choose to look at what's right in any given situation, and become a beacon of love and joy.

Enough Is Enough

The secret to life is to know when enough is enough.

—DR. VINCENT RYAN

This was my father's favorite saying in his final years, and one of the last things he said to me before he died. I was contemplating selling my house and moving to a smaller one, and that was his pronouncement on the subject.

It was kind of ironic, since there he was, a family doctor for forty years, gasping and wheezing over the phone, barely able to speak, dying from smoking too much. But the fact that he learned the lesson late doesn't negate its truth. And it goes straight to the heart of the issue of gratitude: namely, that gratitude makes us feel like we have enough, whereas ingratitude leaves us in a state of deprivation in which we are always looking for something else.

That's why the idea of cultivating "the gratitude attitude" is so popular among twelve-step programs. As Emmet Miller notes in *Gratitude: A Way of Life*, "Gratitude has to do with feeling full, complete, adequate—we have everything we need and deserve; we approach the world with a sense of value." Addictions of all sorts come from a sense of deprivation, a feeling of lack that the user believes can be filled with a substance or activity, whether it's alcohol, drugs, shopping, sex, or food. Caught up in lack, we feed the need but never feel truly satisfied because of course our substance of choice can't fill the lack. Consequently we continue to want more, more, more.

As many people have pointed out, our consumer society owes its very existence to its ability to fuel a sense of never being satisfied. If we were happy about the way we looked, for example, why would we spend billions on cosmetics and plastic surgery? Or on expensive cars that supposedly convey a certain image that we don't have?

An attitude of gratitude gets us off the treadmill and out of the rat race. As we cultivate a true and deep appreciation for what we do have, we realize that our sense of lack is, for the most part, an illusion. No matter our material circumstances, the richness of our soul is ultimately what brings us happiness, not another martini, bigger breasts, or the latest video game. As Lao Tzu proclaimed, "He who knows enough is enough will always have enough."

Always the First Time

Make it new.

—EZRA POUND

I once went to a conference on relationships. Most of the presenters were therapists who had all kinds of elaborate theories about what made good relationships. Then a Buddhist lama got up and said, "I know the secret to keeping love alive. It's simple. All you have to do is act as if you have just met this person and are falling in love. When you meet someone you are interested in, everything they do is wonderful. You love looking at them, hearing what they have to say. Even when they play you country western music, which you hate, you think, 'Well, maybe Tammy Wynette isn't so bad after all.' As time goes on, however, you take the person for granted and fight over Tammy Wynette. So the solution is to see your loved one new again." The therapists were up in arms, proclaiming that such a task was too hard. "Oh," said the lama, "I said it was simple. I didn't say it was easy."

I believe the lama is right. The secret to love—and a sense of joy and gratitude toward all of life—is to see, feel, and hear as if for the First Time. Before the scales of the habitual clouded the brilliant blue sky outside your office window, the tangy juiciness of an orange, or the softness of your loved one's hands. Before you got so used to her kind words, his musical laughter, that they became invisible.

Recently my husband Don had vividly brought home to him the truth of how easy it is to get blinded to the miracles around us. When we first adopted Ana, we couldn't sleep; we were too busy looking into her peaceful face and crying tears of gratitude. Now, a mere four months later, Don, who is home all day with her, finds himself taking her presence for granted, already losing that overwhelming sense of appreciation for her being sent to us. "I get bored," he says, "because it is so much the same, day after day. But her spirit, her presence, is no less a miracle today than it was four months ago, or will be four or forty-years from now. And when I can remember that, I catch myself 'falling asleep' to the miracle, and the awareness wakes me again and my heart once again fills with joy."

When we can live our lives as if it is always the first time—the first time we made love, the first time we gazed upon the face of our beloved, the first time we tasted ice cream, the first time we saw a bird—we won't have to try to experience a sense of gratitude. It will be there, automatically, as a natural response to the beauty and the bounty.

It's OK to Have Good Fortune

There are two ways to live your life.
One is as though nothing is a miracle.
The other is as though everything is
a miracle.

—ALBERT EINSTEIN

Recently someone told me that evolutionary biologist Jerod Diamond wrote the current bestselling book, *Guns, Germs, and Steel,* in answer to an aborigine's question, "Why do you guys have all the stuff?" Diamond set out to understand the historical reasons why, but the moral and spiritual issue is what haunts me.

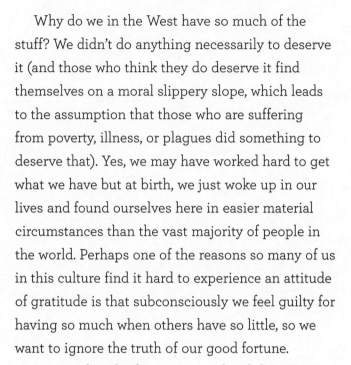

Why do we in the West have so much of the stuff? We didn't do anything necessarily to deserve it (and those who think they do deserve it find themselves on a moral slippery slope, which leads to the assumption that those who are suffering from poverty, illness, or plagues did something to deserve that). Yes, we may have worked hard to get what we have but at birth, we just woke up in our lives and found ourselves here in easier material circumstances than the vast majority of people in the world. Perhaps one of the reasons so many of us in this culture find it hard to experience an attitude of gratitude is that subconsciously we feel guilty for having so much when others have so little, so we want to ignore the truth of our good fortune.

I remember the first time I realized this personally. I was about twelve and writing an essay for Sunday school. I can't remember the question I was supposed to be answering, but I ended up writing about how lucky I was to be living in the affluent United States instead of on the streets of India.

I don't know about you, but that childish realization now makes me pretty uncomfortable. First, it smacks of cultural imperialism; after all, who am I to say that my life is truly better? Just because we in the West have more stuff doesn't mean we are necessarily happier.

On another level, I feel that I must do something important to continue to deserve my good fortune, and nothing can be important enough. At yet another level, it makes me want to ignore and deny my good fortune so that I don't have to feel guilty.

The issues are complex, and ultimately every person born into relative affluence has to define for themselves what their responsibility is. Here, I simply want to ask the question: Is it possible for us in this culture to truly and fully appreciate what we have been given without feeling guilty? If not, perhaps it is our responsibility to acknowledge our guilt, so that it doesn't block our willingness to be grateful.

You Are Worthy

You are a child of the universe, no less than the trees and the stars; you have a right to be here.

—DESIDERATA

My stepdaughter invited a college friend to our house for a week during winter vacation. I did the usual things hosts do for guests: put out clean sheets and towels, made a bouquet of fresh flowers for the bedside table, found out what she liked and didn't like for meals. At dinner, I made polite conversation, inquiring about her interests, her family, her hopes and dreams. At the end of the week, she left, giving no indication of thanks in either word or deed. No note, no present, no phone call.

Now, I didn't entertain her to be thanked, and I wasn't even upset. Rather, I was fascinated about where such a lack of gratitude came from. In talking to my stepdaughter about it, she revealed that she has a hard time with this friend because the young woman has such a low sense of self-esteem. "I spent half my day reassuring her that she looks OK, that she said the right thing, that she is smart and interesting," my stepdaughter complained.

Suddenly I got it—this young woman thinks so poorly of herself that it doesn't even register that other people find her worthy of flowers and good dinners. What I did was invisible to her because she is invisible to herself!

To experience gratitude, you have to be aware that you've been given something—whether it's a beautiful head of hair, a trip to Tahiti, or a great new job—because gratitude is the response of the receiver of a gift. It cannot exist if you don't recognize that you have received a gift, and it can't exist if you don't feel worthy of getting the gift. A lack of self-esteem robs you of the joys of gratitude, because you have nowhere to put all that is being given.

By virtue of simply being alive, we receive gifts all the time—if only a new day, a second (or a one-hundredth second) chance—and we are also worthy simply by virtue of being alive. If you have trouble seeing the gifts in your life, perhaps your self-concept needs strengthening.

Take inspiration from Maya Angelou. In a interview with Oprah Winfrey, she was once asked why, despite the hardships she faced, she never doubted herself. Her answer was that she came to realize that God loved her, and from that point on, she no longer had doubts. Because if God loves her, how could she doubt herself?

You are worthy of all that you receive.

Your Soul Has a Purpose

It is up to you to illumine the earth.

—PHILIPPE VENSIER

Tom Chappell, along with his wife, is the owner of Tom's of Maine, the natural personal care products company. In his audiotape *The Soul of Business*, he describes how, despite his incredible material success (a big house, a huge boat, a very successful business), he woke up one day at age forty-three and realized that he felt disconnected from the company and himself. He considered retiring. Then he decided to go to divinity school to become a minister. There he refound his purpose, coming to see that his ministry was to incorporate into the business practices of Tom's of Maine the values that he believed in deeply, and to help other business-people bring soulfulness into their workplaces as well.

If you want the habit of gratitude to grace your life, it is essential that you, like Tom Chappell, develop the belief that you are here on Earth to fulfill some purpose that only you can offer to the

world. You are an amazingly rare, totally nonrep-
licable individual with talents and gifts that the
world anxiously needs. The more that you experience the truth of your uniqueness and beauty, the
more you will feel gratitude for your particular gifts,
and the more you will be able to deliver those gifts.

Unfortunately, not many of us were born to
parents who nurtured our individuality, honored
our gifts, or helped us recognize our purpose. So as
adults we may find it difficult to love ourselves in
a wholehearted way that fosters a deep and quiet
sense of gratitude for ourselves. In *The Woman's
Book of Spirit*, Sue Patton Thoele offers the following meditation:

"It may help to realize the value of gratitude
toward ourselves if we were to visualize our heart
as a delicate treasure, hand-blown from the rarest
ethereal glass. A treasure valuable beyond imagining—fragile, irreplaceable, priceless, and ancient.
There is no other like it—infinitely precious, exist-
ing before time and after infinity.

"In reality, we were entrusted with such an
inexplicable treasure when we were given the gift
of life. . . .

"With your eyes closed, very gently put your hands over your heart and allow your breath to tenderly flow in and out of it. When you feel ready, ask to be given a symbol for your heart. Hold that symbol that you see or sense as carefully as you would a priceless Fabergé egg. Beholding the wonder of your symbol, allow gratitude to flow through you, permeating the very cells of your being. Make a commitment with yourself to cherish and appreciate your heart-self."

The Solution in the Problem

People are always blaming their circumstances for what they are. I don't believe in circumstances.
The people who get on in this world are the people who get up and look for the circumstances they want and if they can't find them, make them.

—GEORGE BERNARD SHAW

A therapist I know was treating a woman who'd had a serious stroke and was suffering from aphasia, difficulty in speaking. She didn't seem too troubled by it, but her family considered it a great tragedy. As a young Jewish woman, her verbal ability was a great gift—it had even saved her life. She spoke five languages and survived the Holocaust by becoming a translator for the Nazis in a concentration camp. After the war, she moved to the United States and supported her family teaching foreign languages. Now she struggled for words and her adult children were constantly jumping in to "help" her by filling in her words.

The stroke had changed her in other ways too. Cold and distant as a mother, the stroke had left her very physically affectionate, and she constantly touched her children. However, they were so caught up in the loss of her speaking ability that they didn't recognize that what they were now receiving from her was the kind of affection that they had longed for all their lives.

The therapist taught them that whenever they found themselves frustrated by her lack of verbal acuity, instead of trying to fill in her words, to take a breath and really notice her loving them through her touch. This allowed the woman to have the space she needed to speak, and the children to appreciate the love that was coming from their mother.

The point of this "trick" is to use a source of frustration as a trigger to cultivate an attitude of gratitude. Is there something in your life that you find terribly annoying or difficult? Is there some hidden gift in the annoying situation that you, like the children in this story, can focus on to create an opportunity for gratitude?

For me it's standing in line. I absolutely hate to "waste" time; I live my life at a frenetic pace and don't want anything to get in my way of doing all I have to get done in a day. Until recently, I was the person in the line huffing and rolling my eyes at the wait, jiggling and looking at my watch every few seconds. And when I finally made it to the counter, I was too aggravated from having to wait to be pleasant to the person on the other side of the counter. But since life is full of lines, I finally decided to change my approach. Instead of being annoyed, I decided to see waiting in line as a

wonderful opportunity to slow down, to take a few conscious breaths, become aware of my body, and release as much muscle tension as I could. The waits are as long as ever—but now I am grateful for the chance to stop.

The Time Is Now

We can spend a whole lifetime enjoying various benefits and not appreciate their value until we are deprived of them. How many lovers boldly contemplate separation, fondly imagining that they have had enough of the beloved. And yet as soon as they actually experience separation, they burn up with longing.

—JAMI

Boy, do I recognize myself in Sufi Jami's quote! Retroactive gratitude I call it—realizing after something is over or someone is gone that I really appreciated what I had, but wasn't aware of it until it was gone. Good health, the smile of a loved one, a job that allowed for creativity and self-expression—the list of what we might have taken for granted is endless.

Failing to appreciate what we had until it's "too late" leads to regret, one of the most insidious negative feelings there is. Regret is a poison that keeps us in the past: If only I had told him more often I was thankful for all he gave me, maybe he would not have left me; if only I had been more appreciative of my legs before I got hit by the car . . . if only, if only. Our minds spin around, creating story upon story of how life could have been better if we had taken less for granted.

Whenever I find myself swirling around in a fog of retroactive gratitude, I do two things. First, I take time to consciously thank the person or thing I have belatedly discovered my gratitude for. If the person is alive, I thank them via letter or phone call. If not, I send a mental thanks, as I do for a situation I am grateful for. Second, I take a hard look at my current life, at the things I might be taking for granted right now.

While we can never know if being grateful in the moment would have created a different outcome, what is for sure is that the more we give thanks now for what we do have, the fewer regrets we will have in the future, no matter what happens. Maybe you can't tell your sister who just died how grateful you were for her presence in your life, but right now you can tell your husband, your child, and your best friend what they mean to you.

Let the fact of our regret send us into the world with ever more appreciation for the gifts we have been given, and a commitment to communicate that appreciation as often as possible.

The Joy of Living

It was then I learned that gratitude is the best feeling I would ever have, the ultimate joy of living. It was better than sex, better than winning the lottery, better than watching your daughter graduate from college, better and deeper than any other feeling; it is perhaps the genesis of all other really good feelings in the human repertoire.

—LEWIS SMEDES, AFTER ALMOST DYING

In *A Pretty Good Person*, Lewis Smedes, a professor of theology and ethics at Fuller Theological Seminary, tells the story of collapsing in his Minnesota apartment on a "frightfully cold December morning. . . .

"My lungs it turned out, had been spattered by a buckshot of blood clots; and for a couple of days at the hospital I tilted in death's direction. On the fourth day a benign Norwegian physician by the name of Hans Engman leaned over my bed and congratulated me on surviving the twenty-to-one odds that medical statistics had stacked up against me. . . .

"A couple of nights later—in the moody hush that settles on a hospital room at two o'clock in the morning, alone, with no drugs in me to set me up for it—I was seized with a frenzy of gratitude. . . . I blessed the Lord above for the almost unbearable goodness of being alive on this good earth in this good body at this present time."

In doing research for this book, it was amazing to me how many people related a similar story— that it took a brush with death to awaken them to a sense of gratitude. I read about how car accidents, cancer experiences, boating mishaps, and other life-threatening difficulties were wake-up calls to live with more thankfulness for the ordinary things of life. These weren't intellectual decisions; rather, each person was overwhelmed with a tremendous feeling of gratitude, as Lewis Smedes describes, and from that feeling made a pledge to cultivate gratefulness on a daily basis.

My question is this: Do you need to almost die to experience the joy available in this moment? Or is it possible, right now, to tap into the amazingly wonderful fact that you are alive, breathing in and breathing out, able to take in the world through your senses, able to smile to a stranger, caress a loved one, touch the soft down of a baby's cheek? We do not need to almost die to feel the wonderful warm bath of gratitude. In any moment, we can experience the world as new again, and touch the joyful ecstasy those who have gone through near-death experiences relate.

Think for a moment of something you almost lost but didn't—a friend in an argument, your car that was stolen but then abandoned, a breast, your life. Does your heart naturally swell in thanksgiving for their continued presence in your life?

THE ATTITUDES OF GRATITUDE

An Ever-Increasing Spiral

As I express my gratitude, I become more deeply aware of it. And the greater my awareness, the greater my need to express it. What happens here is a spiraling ascent, a process of growth in ever-expanding circles around a steady center.

—BROTHER DAVID STEINDL-RAST

"My Russian grandmother was my greatest teacher in gratitude," a coworker recently told me. "We were very poor and I often would complain about not having this or that. Any time we went anywhere, she would use whatever happened as a lesson in giving thanks. We'd walk down the streets of New York and see a man without legs begging for food, and she would say, 'Now you send up a prayer right now to God thanking him for your legs and for the food in your belly.' She wouldn't do it to feel superior to the man or to make me feel guilty, but to teach me that around us every day are ways

ATTITUDES OF GRATITUDE

to remind ourselves of the bounty we have, no matter what our circumstances, and the more we give thanks, the more likely it is that the blessings will continue. For years in my adolescence, I rejected her teaching. But lately I've begun to notice that the more I give thanks, the better my life goes. When I become ungrateful, things tend to fall apart."

A lot of the recent writing on gratitude makes it sound like some kind of insurance policy, as if the reason to feel grateful is to make sure that good things will continue to come our way. That feels spiritually materialistic to me, like praying for a pink Cadillac or a mink stole. True gratitude is a natural response to the miracle of life as we experience it moment to moment, a sense of abundance from the heart that is independent of our desires for the future.

That said, it does seem to be true that whatever we focus on tends to increase. Have you ever noticed that if you learn a new word you suddenly hear it everywhere? Or your friend introduces you to blue lobelia and you suddenly notice it blooming all over?

Exactly why this happens is something of a mystery, but I believe it's because everything is around us all the time. We are choosing, mostly unconsciously, to notice certain things and not others because we just cannot pay attention to everything. As we change what we pay attention to, we notice that more. Scientists have proposed that something more amazing is at work—that reality is open to the mind's causal influence and is, in the words of David L. Cooperider, "often profoundly created through our anticipatory images, values, plans, intentions, beliefs and the like." This suggests that we actually participate in creating what happens to us by the power of our positive or negative imagery.

In either case, the more we are grateful, the more we will have to be grateful for. Even if nothing more or better happens, our eyes are opened to the gifts that were always there. As Susan Jeffers notes, "When we focus on abundance, our life feels abundant; when we focus on lack, our life feels lacking. It is purely a matter of focus."

Start Where You Are

If you haven't got all the things you want,
be grateful for the things you don't have
that you don't want.

—ANONYMOUS

Sometimes we are in such a negative state that the
only way we can connect to a sense of gratefulness
is to count all the bad things that aren't happening
to us: well, the dog didn't get hit by a car today; I
don't have Alzheimer's yet; my kid didn't pierce her
nose today; an earthquake didn't strike.

Counting blessings that are blessings by virtue
of their not having struck, the more outrageous the
better, is a great mood-elevator. By the time you
recite your list to a loved one or friend, you should
be feeling a whole lot better.

But there is a serious aspect to this as well.
When you really think about it, isn't it wonderful
that the tornado didn't strike? Isn't it great that
the house didn't burn down? (It's a real possibility.
Three of my closest friends have had their homes
or businesses burn to the ground.) Sometimes we

need to look at what hasn't befallen us to wake ourselves up to the joys of our ordinary life.

Often we arrive at this place by hearing about the misfortunes of others; "Oh, thank God it wasn't my child in that car crash"; "I'm so grateful that it's not my husband who's losing his job"; "Think of all those poor people who lost their homes." Such reactions are human nature, I suppose, and yet it would be wonderful if we didn't need the sorrows of other people to remind us of the blessings in our own lives. Rather, if we consciously count our blessings on a daily basis, including those that are blessings by virtue of their not happening, instead of experiencing a sense of grateful relief when we hear about someone else's misfortune perhaps we will be spurred into the action that comes from an awakened sense of compassion.

CHAPTER 4

The Practices of Gratitude

Beginning to tune in to even the minutest feelings of . . . gratitude softens us. . . . If we begin to acknowledge these moments and cherish them . . . then no matter how fleeting and tiny this good heart may seem, it will gradually, at its own speed, expand.

—PEMA CHÖDRÖN

Now we come to the next stage of our journey, which is where we begin to put our attitudes into action. Here we don't just feel grateful, but we move to express our feelings of gratefulness in a variety of ways that enrich our lives and the lives of those around us. This is where we truly ripen as souls, for it is easy to pay lip service to the idea of gratitude and not take the final step of embodying it. But when we begin to practice gratitude, we create a powerful resonance between our thoughts and our actions, and our souls shine forth in all their brillance.

Exercise Daily

Your future depends on many things, but mostly on you.

—FRANK TYGER

Even though I have spent the last twenty-five years as an editor and a writer, I am continually amazed that writing is a muscle that must be exercised. When I or my authors do it every day, it comes

relatively easily, just like running a mile does for a marathoner. When too much time has passed since I last sat down in front of the computer, my brain is creaky like an athlete coming back after an injury. Once, when I had not written for a month, I despaired that I could ever do it again.

The same is true for fostering any attitude. The more you do it, the easier it is to do. In fact, I'm convinced that this is the difference between an optimist and a pessimist. A pessimist is someone who has exercised the muscles of negativity and lack till they are strongly habitual, while an optimist is a person who has developed thankfulness and a can-do attitude until these are second nature. We all have the choice of which muscles we want to strengthen. With practice, we can become joy-filled participants in the game of life, thankful to do our part and relishing in the sheer pleasure of play.

When I think of someone who really exercises her gratitude muscles, I think of Peris. She's the kind of person who calls her friends out of the blue to thank them for being in her life. She comes from a large Croatian family, replete with all kinds of screwball uncles and zany aunts, the kind of family

many of us would run from. Listening to her stories, you begin to appreciate your own quirky family members in the same way she does. Recently I
called her to ask her about gratitude. She didn't get
back to me right away, and when she finally did, she
said my call had reminded her that she hadn't been
feeling very thankful lately and was grateful for the
wake-up.

Like Peris, you have to practice or the muscle
will wither. Developing the muscle of gratitude is
just like exercising any other. At first it will seem
weird, awkward, perhaps even hard to do. But if you
keep at it every day, soon you won't even have to
think about it.

Whether you keep a gratitude journal or start a
practice of thinking about all you are grateful for
as you drive to or from work, creating some daily
ritual really helps build the muscle. Only you know
what will work best for you—a file on your computer,
a beautiful blank book, an audiotape in your car.
Whichever format you pick, make a commitment
to list ten things every day that you are grateful
for. Pretty soon it will be second nature. Here's the
beginning of my list: "I didn't get in a car accident;

my computer worked; my baby is healthy; it stopped raining; I had steak for dinner; my house is warm and dry; my sister called. . . ."

Choose Gratefulness "In Spite Of"

*As you wander on through life, sister/
brother, whatever be your goal, keep your
eye upon the donut, and not upon the hole.*

—SIGN IN THE MAYFLOWER COFFEE SHOP, CHICAGO

Bestselling author Iyanla Venzant, who penned such inspirational books as *Acts of Faith* and *One Day My Soul Just Opened*, has lived the prototypical rags-to-riches story. A former welfare recipient, she was about forty when her life began to turn around. Through it all, she claims, her sense of gratitude kept her going. "I'm grateful for everything," she says, "from being homeless to sitting in a half-million-dollar house."

This remarkable woman is pointing to something very important about gratitude—that we can

experience it even "in spite of" something else: that our friend is lying in a hospital dying, that millions of people are starving as you read this book, that our own lives have trials and tribulations that might be sorely testing us.

We can't wait until everything is OK—with us or with the rest of the world—to feel thankful, or we will never experience it at all. "The world is too bent for unshadowed joy," Lewis Smedes points out, and so we must catch and kiss our joy as it flies by, even in the midst of sorrow or suffering. This is not to imply that we deny suffering, but just that we not allow our suffering to blind us to the beauty and joy that surrounds us no matter what else is going on.

It's a matter of where you choose to put your attention. Try the following experiments: Pick one morning and stop every hour on the hour and notice what went wrong in that time period. The traffic was terrible and you were late to work; the weather was gloomy and cold; your boss complained about the project you've worked so hard on. That afternoon, stop every hour on the hour and notice what went right: An old friend called out of the blue; the sun came out; you did an excellent job on the sales letter.

Did you feel more alive in the morning or in the afternoon?

Revel in the Ordinary

Normal day, let me be aware of the treasure you are. Let me learn from you, love you, bless you before you depart. Let me not pass you by in quest of some rare and perfect tomorrow. Let me hold you while I may, for it may not always be so. One day I shall dig my nails into the earth, or bury my face in the pillow, or stretch myself taut, or raise my hands to the sky and want, more than all the world, your return.

—MARY JEAN IRON

It's hard to appreciate the ordinary, except in contrast to something hard or challenging. I am always reminded of the truth of this when I've been sick. When I am well, I take my physical being for granted. I don't particularly notice how I feel; I'm simply not

aware of it. But when I've been sick and begin to feel better, I am filled with immense gratitude for how good it feels not to be sick—not to have an aching head, a burning throat, leaden muscles and joints. I feel exactly as I normally do, but now I notice how great that is.

Other people experience this sensation from a close call in a car or plane, an almost-bankruptcy, anything that shakes us out of complacency and wakes us to the wonder of our ordinary existence.

The trick, of course, is to learn how to have that awareness without having to be sick, almost lose your house, or get hurt in a car crash. One way to do it is to pick an ordinary task, something you do every day, and decide that just for today, you will do it with awareness. It can be anything—washing dishes, chopping vegetables, making the bed. Instead of doing it while thinking about something else, such as the dinner that still needs to be made or how mad you are at the driver who cut you off, you actually pay attention to the task itself rather than being on automatic pilot. Notice the high-pitched whirring of the vacuum cleaner, the hard-yet-soft feel of the ribbed hose in your hand, the

sight of the white dog hairs against the hardwood floor as they are sucked into the vacuum. . . .

This kind of awareness practice, the more specific the better, is great for fostering a sense of appreciation for the ordinary. As Rick Field notes, "When we pay attention, whatever we are doing—whether it be cooking, cleaning or making love—is transformed. . . . We begin to notice details and textures that we never noticed before; everyday life becomes clearer, sharper, and at the same time more spacious." Our eyes are opened once again to the miracles of the absolutely ordinary and joy fills our hearts.

What Do You Really Need?

The grand essentials to happiness in this life are something to do, something to love, and something to hope for.

—JOSEPH ADDISON

A friend of mine who has health problems recently decided to sell her big, beautiful house in the

country and move to a small condo in the city. It is easier for her to manage the day-to-day basics of life in a smaller home, close to public transportation, and the financial pressure is much lighter. But she's been finding it quite difficult to let go of all the beautiful attributes of her big house, particularly since she's discovered that her budget won't allow for certain amenities she was counting on. "Yesterday," she confided to me, "I found out that I can't have the French doors I had my heart set on. They're just too expensive. I started to feel terrible, but then I asked myself, honestly, do you need French doors? The answer of course was No, and I felt much better."

When we focus on what we truly need, as opposed to what we might like or want, life gets much simpler, and it's much easier to feel grateful. Because, when it comes right down to it, there's not a whole lot that we really need. Do we need a cherry-red Jeep? A trip to Barbados? What about a television? A garden? Time off with family? A job that gives you a sense of purpose?

It's helpful to look around and figure out what you need to be happy. If you really think about it,

it's not a long list: food, shelter, rest, loved ones, something meaningful to do. That's about it. All the rest of the stuff of life are wants. Important wants, but wants nonetheless. For example, at the top of my "need" list is a hot tub. I go in at least once a day, often twice, and it helps my back and my temperament a lot. But I lived for years without one and got along just fine, so on reflection I would have to say that it's not a true need.

My friend's remark about the French doors has been incredibly helpful in cultivating an attitude of gratitude. Now, every time I get caught up in wanting something and bemoaning the fact that I can't have it, I ask myself, "But do I need this to be happy?" It's amazing how often the answer is No. Give it a try yourself right now.

Do the Work of Forgiveness

There are many ways to victimize people. One way is to convince them that they are victims.

—KAREN HWANG

Nothing blocks feelings of gratitude more than anger and resentment. That's why the practice of gratitude requires the work of forgiveness. We can't feel grateful to our parents for what we received from them when we are still angry about their abuse, self-involvement, insensitivity, alcoholism, or neglect. Nor can we receive the gifts of a relationship that has ended when we still feel hurt over betrayal, angry over deceit, sorrowful over abandonment.

Nor should we. Trying to force ourselves to feel grateful when such strong negative feelings exist only compounds the injury. We have been hurt. Let's not deny our woundedness on top of everything else. Healing, in the form of acknowledging the grievance and grieving the loss or wound, needs to happen first.

However, there comes a time in the process of emotional resolution for forgiveness. For only forgiveness can move us out of the victim stance and free us to move on. Depending on the kind of wound you have suffered, this may be deep psychological and spiritual work. No one can talk you into it. No one can do it for you. Only you can come to the place where you want to forgive.

What helps the forgiveness process is to understand that resentment is a second-hand emotion, a cover for underlying feelings that have never been expressed. That's why it is useful to do a practice called "A Damage Report." In a letter (that you never send) to your abuser, write down all the effects the wounding had on you, in as much detail as you possibly can. Don't hold back. Then create a boundary, something like: I will get up and leave the room if someone is verbally abusing me; or, I will not stay with anyone who is abusing drugs. This will help you develop trust that you will protect yourself against such circumstances and people in the future. Then write a note of forgiveness to yourself for not having stated your boundary before, and a note of thanks to the other person for the learning, so that it won't happen again.

If you really take the time to express fully your needs and pain and state your new boundary, chances are you'll begin to be grateful for the lessons the wounding has taught you, whether it's to stand up for yourself, to be kinder toward others, to stop drinking, whatever. At some point you realize that you are a better, stronger, more loving person

than you might have been if you hadn't been so hurt, and you recognize the gift in your particular suffering. In that moment, you move from victim to victor, from victor to venerated teacher.

Forgiveness leads to gratitude, and not just gratitude in general but, in a beautifully healing movement, to an outpouring of appreciation for the very things that caused such pain in the first place. Thus is our suffering redeemed.

Practice Wonderment

*Oh, for the wonder that bubbles
into my soul.*

—D. H. LAWRENCE

Recently I took my one-year-old daughter to the zoo for the first time. Her eyes almost popped out of her head when she saw an elephant. And when I gave her her first scoop of ice cream, her joy knew no bounds. Her little body wriggled, her eyes sparkled, and she brought out the biggest smile. The truth is elephants are amazing creatures, and ice

cream is just as delicious the one-thousandth time as the first. But we adults have lost our wonderment, and so we can't appreciate elephants and ice cream as much.

In wonderment, children are our greatest teachers. Wonder is a natural state, one that we often lose track of as we become numb to life. Since wonderment is the willingness to be surprised by life, and gratitude springs from wonderment, to practice gratefulness we need to let life surprise us, with a glorious sunset, a luxurious back rub, a mysterious phone call, or the kindness of a stranger. The problem with adulthood is that we become jaded: Oh yes, another great sunset, another fabulous dinner, another birthday present.

We can recapture our sense of wonderment at any moment. All it takes is to open our senses and let the world come into us anew. Try it for one minute. First, listen to the sounds around you: perhaps an airplane is overhead. Isn't it amazing that airplanes can fly? It doesn't seem possible. What kinds of scents are in the air? I can smell jasmine. Isn't it amazing that so many flowers have such distinctive scents?

134

Now turn to your sense of sight. Really notice what's around you: the grain in the wooden door; the black letters against the white page, the bright yellow bananas in the bowl. Isn't it amazing that you can see? Isn't it fascinating to wonder if everyone can see yellow the same way as you? Isn't it marvelous that you can have a banana even though they grow thousands of miles away?

We can touch wonder in every moment as we slow down and perceive the world around us as if for the first time. And when we contact wonder, we know thankfulness for the most ordinary, extraordinary things of life.

Don't Compare

Life begets life. Energy creates energy.
It is by spending oneself that one
becomes rich.

—SARAH BERNHARDT

Driving home the other day, I heard on the radio that as the stock market went up, so did the salaries

of corporate bosses who take stock options as part
of their compensation. Last year, the head of Disney
made $10 million, another guy in L.A. made $45
million, and that's not even considering Bill Gates.
I could feel my blood turning green with envy, and
all sense of gratitude for my own life—that I have a
wonderful, loving family, close friends, a beautiful
house, fundamentally good health—went flying
out the window. "If only I could have just one of
their many millions," I thought, "then my life would
be happy."

The truth is, of course, that happiness is an
inside job and, beyond the subsistence level, money
truly has very little to do with our happiness. But
most of us are convinced that money can indeed
buy happiness. The universality of that feeling
struck me a few years ago when I read about a
study that asked people how much money they
thought they needed to be happy. Everyone, no
matter what they made, thought they needed more.
People who made $20,000 thought $30,000 would
do it; folks at $45,000 were convinced $65,000 was
the magic number, people at $100,000 were sure
$200,000 was it. The only thing that changed was

that as people's incomes grew, their magic number grew exponentially (proving like nothing else that the "gimme hole" only grows through feeding). I realized then that there is something in human nature—well, at least in contemporary Western human nature—that will always long for more and envy those who have it, and the only way to deal with that trait is to acknowledge it: Oh, there you are again, and then turn our attention back to what matters.

Here's a practice for dealing with envy. Spend one day with one pocket of change and one empty pocket. Each time you find yourself envious of someone, put a coin in the empty pocket and ask yourself, "What is there that I am noticing in the other person that I want to find in myself?" (Because you wouldn't notice it if it weren't already in you.) If it's money, is it the freedom? The chance to play that money buys? A sense of security? Whatever it is—more play, a sense of security, free time—you can work on getting more of it in your life, no matter the circumstances.

I can choose to spend my time envying Bill Gates, the housewife who doesn't have to work because her wealthy lawyer husband provides for all her needs,

and the person down the street who just inherited a large estate from his mother, or I can begin to understand what I am really longing for in myself.

I use envy as a trigger to remembering that I want to do a better job of giving myself away, as Sarah Bernhardt counsels, so that I will experience a true sense of richness no matter what my material resources. I can't keep the green-eyed monster from rearing its ugly head from time to time, but I can use its appearance to rededicate myself to using myself fully on behalf of the world as a whole. The feeling of abundance—great fullness—that doing the work our soul is here to do is better than any old million dollars.

Transform Expectations into No Matter Whats

It seems to me that we often, almost sulkily, reject the good that God offers us because, at the moment, we expected some other good.

—C. S. LEWIS

THE PRACTICES OF GRATITUDE

138

The most ungrateful person I know is an older woman who can't see the beauty of her life because she is so bitter that it didn't turn out the way she thought it should. She has a lovely home and garden, healthy, bright, successful children, a fifty-year marriage, and the means and health to travel. No one in her immediate family has died or been seriously ill; she's never known poverty or lack; she is, from all external measures, highly privileged, with much to be grateful for. And yet all of what she has is completely invisible to her because it somehow doesn't match the picture of what she expected. Her kids don't live close enough or visit often enough; she wishes there was even more money; her marriage isn't as loving as she desires. Her ingratitude is a self-fulfilling prophecy, for the more she complains, the more lonely and isolated she finds herself as friends and family grow weary of her moaning.

To me, this acquaintance is an important teacher in the practice of gratitude—a vivid example of how expectations can create blinders so that we can't even see the true blessings of our lives. Expectations are the killers of gratitude and joy:

If you expect to live in the Taj Mahal, your cozy little cottage will feel pretty awful; if you expect your son to become a doctor, you can't appreciate him for the fine bodyworker that he is; if you focus on how you are going to be miserable without a BMW, your trusty, rusty Toyota that reliably gets you around will only bring you misery.

Having hopes, dreams, and visions for the future are one thing; it's important to have goals and schemes pulling us into the future. But we need to be careful that such envisioning doesn't get in the way of appreciating the things we have in the here and now. Let's not miss the beauty of our actual lives while we're lusting after a mythical perfect life.

If we expect someone or something outside ourselves to make us happy, we lose our power. The truth is we can't count on anything except our ability to choose how to respond to what happens to us. One way to counteract the tendency to look outside ourselves for happiness is to practice No Matter What. Before you go into a situation, ask yourself, "What is it that I can learn, accomplish, or experience here, no matter what happens?" Let's say you have to give a speech and are nervous about

how it will be received. Your No Matter What might be, "No matter what, I want to experience a sense of peace while talking. As I look out into the audience, I'll remember to breathe and notice that at my core there is peace." Afterwards, no matter what else happened—that people appeared bored, or no one came up to thank you—you can still appreciate yourself for having kept your commitment to experience peacefulness.

When we practice No Matter What, we are no longer hooked by expectations to externals—other people, other events—but are free to choose what we will focus on to make us happy.

Develop a Good Memory

Gratitude is the memory of the heart;
therefore forget not to say often, I have
all I ever enjoyed.

—LYDIA CHILD

Sometimes life is so challenging, so painful, that it is plain impossible to feel grateful for anything that

ATTITUDES OF GRATITUDE

is going on. At such moments, it's nice to have a reservoir of contentment to fall back on, a storehouse of joyful memories to open and hold onto as you navigate through the dark night of the soul.

A good memory doesn't just work for really tough times. It also helps to smooth over the little bumps and glitches of ordinary life, particularly in relationships. When I find myself annoyed with something my husband is saying, for instance, if I can remember the piece of angel food cake he brought me as a surprise yesterday while I was working, my annoyance melts as my gratitude is engaged. A good memory also helps, for example, when you find yourself angry at a coworker for failing to meet a deadline. Recalling with gratitude how often she has come through for you in the past, graciously let her off the hook.

A good memory keeps us from losing our perspective, from being so caught up in the work of the here and now that we forget the larger bounty of our lives. I'm not suggesting that we should deny our suffering or ignore the problems in our lives, just that we can balance them with joy and

peacefulness by remembering moments, events, and people that we are grateful for.

What are the things in your life that, looking back, you are most thankful for? Notice what comes up without your reaching for it. This practice is not about making a laundry list but of allowing yourself to notice what really sticks with you. These are your Highlights of Happiness: the birth of your son, recovery from a serious illness, a certain way the light falls in your bedroom—whatever they are, they are your precious moments to be taken out and savored any time you need them.

Take Time to Smell the Roses

It's good to have an end to journey toward; but it's the journey that matters, in the end.

—URSULA K. LEGUIN

The practice of gratitude requires that you slow down long enough to notice what is right in front of your nose. If you are speeding through the day,

chances are you are overlooking the blessings that are all around you. No matter what our circumstances, we can slow down enough to notice and give thanks to our breath going in and out, the food we are about to eat, the book we are reading, the kindness of the stranger we bumped into. As we take the time to open our five senses to the world around us, we won't miss the shooting star, the life-altering words, the tiny blue violets. And our lives will be enriched by the bounty all around us.

We've all been told to stop and smell the roses a million times; we forget it as promptly as we hear it. So what will actually get us to do it?

The trick is to use the goings-on in daily life as triggers. In his book *Stopping*, David Kundtz suggests the practice of Stillpoints, stops for a very brief time, that are made in the "unfilled moments in life": while waiting for the microwave to heat your coffee, standing in line, walking from one appointment to the next, sitting at a red light. Sitting or standing, you "stop, breathe, and remember." Stop, notice a breath in and a breath out, and remember. The remembering can be any message that is powerful and important for you: that you

are loved, that you are filled with peace and joy, that you have plenty of time to do what you have to, that you can notice the world around you in this moment. If you are trying to increase your sense of gratitude, perhaps your message can be something like, "I notice the gifts surrounding me in this moment."

David suggests that you do Stillpoints many times a day in order to increase your sense of inner peace and awareness. What trigger would work best for you? What will work best is something that causes you to pause anyway, and that you experience several times a day, like a red light or a bathroom break. For the monks and nuns at Plum Village in France, it is the telephone. They notice three breaths before they answer the phone. It doesn't matter what you choose, only that you begin to practice.

Focus on What's Right

Thank God for what doesn't need healing.

—JOAN BORYSENKO

We are so incredibly well trained to notice what's wrong in any given relationship, work situation, or experience that it's easy to overlook what's right. That's not surprising, because our entire education system trains us to notice flaws and mistakes: in school, the wrong answers are marked, not the right ones. In relationships, we spend a lot of time, energy, and money, often with the help of therapists, working on fixing what's wrong. At work, we study our failures and mistakes for hidden clues so that we can prevent them from happening again.

But what if we have it backward? What would we be like now if all the answers we got correct on every test had been marked? What if we spent as much energy in relationships noticing and appreciating the other person's gifts and talents and the strengths and beauty of the relationship itself as we do exposing and dealing with its flaws? What if, at work, we spent an equal amount of time looking at what is working and how we can do more of that as we do analyzing what's wrong?

An "asset focus"—noticing and appreciating, as Joan Borysenko puts it, what doesn't need healing, is an incredibly powerful tool for creating

connection, fostering creative thinking, and over-coming obstacles. I saw this most powerfully at an office retreat in which we honored the twelve people who worked at Conari Press. We went around the room, focusing on one person at a time. The rules were simple: Anyone who wished to could say what they appreciated about that person; no one had to speak; no one could interrupt or interject; and the receiver had to just listen without comment.

We had allotted an hour for the practice; it ended up taking three, because there was so much we wanted to say about each person. People laughed and cried. By the end, the sense of cama-raderie, connection, and team were the strongest I ever felt. The next day, we came up with some of the best book ideas we've ever thought of. I still remember vividly what people said.

You can do this with any group—work team, church group, in your own family. I really encour-age you to try it. It's one of the most magical things I've ever done.

Be Willing to Embrace What Shows Up

I have learned, in whatsoever state I am in, therewith to be content.

—SAINT PAUL

I once studied with a group that believed life is an active force at work on an individual. They believed that for every person, there are three circles of influence: you, other people, and life itself. All three are interconnected and interpenetrating: just as you influence and are influenced by those around you, so does life influence and is influenced by you. (Many people believe that God operates in a similar way.)

I found the idea quite reassuring. Instead of feeling alone in an uncaring, random universe that threw trouble my way willy-nilly, I could take comfort in feeling that there was some two-way relationship between life and me. Which might also mean that there was a good reason that certain things showed up and not others. This made it easier for

me to be content with what happens in my life, rather than always yearning for something else.

Such contentment is important to cultivate, because life has a way of throwing us curves: We want a Persian cat, but a stray lands at our doorstep; we want to have a baby but are plagued by infertility; we want that fabulous new job, but are passed over. Unless we embrace what shows up in our lives, we will never get the benefits of the lessons life is trying to teach us: We'll never love the mutt, adopt a baby, or be available for the even better job.

It is only by being grateful for what is that we experience contentment, and it is contentment with what is that makes us happy in the moment—and available to whatever else life has in store for us.

Try the following practice for a week. In the course of your daily life, whenever you encounter something that is not your idea of a good thing, ask yourself, "If everything that is happening is right, how is this right?" What's right about the fight with your mother, the fender-bender, your aching back? Without negating what's wrong, ask yourself what function or need is the event serving? Maybe what's right about the fight is that you are learning to say

No; maybe the fender-bender is a wake-up call that
you are too stressed out; maybe your aching back
is a reminder that your body wants some exercise.
Understand the message so that the lesson won't
have to be learned again. At the end of the week,
reflect on the experience. What changed in you as a
consequence of looking for what's right?

Look for the Hidden Blessings
of Difficult Situations

*Some people once brought a blind man
to Jesus and asked him, "Rabbi, who
sinned, this man or his parents, that
he was born blind?" . . . And Jesus
answered, "It was not that this man
sinned, or his parents, but that the
words of God might be manifest in
him." He told them not to look for why
the suffering came but to listen for
what the suffering could teach them.*

—WAYNE MULLER

Gratitude is an all-out experience. It's cheating to be grateful only for the good things that happen and to shun the bad. This isn't to say that we want bad things to happen to us, just that if we can be grateful for the soul-lessons inherent in the difficulties that befall us, then our souls will be able to grow and mature. Otherwise, we never progress, because we fail to use the hardships that dog us to become more loving, more patient, more present, more kind.

The people whom I admire most in the world say without reservation that the hardest things they had to face—cancer, the death of a child, a bankruptcy, or job loss—had been their greatest teachers and that they were grateful for the lessons. For me it has been dealing with chronic pain.

When I was a senior in college I hurt my back. It was the first time my body ever betrayed me. Until then, I always considered it just a handy container to take my mind where it wanted to go. But suddenly I couldn't move, and I had to pay attention to it. Eventually I spent over a year in bed.

It's been twenty years since then, and my back continues to be one of my greatest teachers. I've

learned a lot about patience (a hard lesson for me!)
and impermanence (just because it hurts like hell
today doesn't mean it will tomorrow). I've learned
the value of physical discipline ("No time to do
those boring back exercises?" my body says. "I'll
show you!"). I've learned that I can't push myself
beyond limits that often I still don't recognize until
after I've exceeded them. That even doing everything "right" is no guarantee I'll be free from pain.
I've learned to let go of my wanting it to be better,
and I've learned about how much I still exist even if
I am able to do absolutely nothing. Now, in theory,
I could have learned these things some other way,
and perhaps I might have. But the truth of my life is
that I have learned them through chronic pain—and
I am grateful for the lessons, if not for the pain.

Right now, write down the ten hardest or most
terrible things that ever happened to you. As you
look over the list, can you see the gifts that each of
them brought?

Metaphysical teacher Daniel T. Peralta suggests
that when you are suffering from some difficulty
whose blessing is invisible to you, you say the following prayer: "I am willing to see the gift in this

experience. May the lessons be revealed to me, and may I become stronger and clearer."

Teach Gratitude to Your Young Ones

Celebrate what you want to see more of.

—TOM PETERS

Many of us in the baby-boom generation, once we were grown, rebelled against "Emily Post, pinky-in-the-air"-type manners. Because we rejected the phony, pro forma "Now what do you say to Mrs. So-and-So?" style of gratitude, lots of us neglected to teach our children how to connect to a true sense of gratefulness. As a result, the younger generations seem to have an overinflated sense of entitlement that blocks any sense of gratitude.

I think our neglect of this important aspect of spiritual guidance also comes from having been "shoulded" so much in our childhoods. How many of us were told we should eat our peas because "children were starving in China (or Armenia or India)"?

How many of us were told we should be grateful because we had a bicycle and running shoes and a lovely bedroom and so many other kids around the world have nothing except bare dirt? As I mentioned before, such remarks only serve to make us feel guilty, and guilt just makes us want to avoid whatever is provoking it.

As recipients of such training, we already know a lot about what doesn't help foster an attitude of gratitude in children. But what does work? Not surprisingly, the same things that work for adults—teaching our kids an asset focus and a conscious counting of their blessings without a guilt trip.

When you're helping your children with homework, if they are having trouble with something break the task into parts and ask them to figure out what part they already know how to do. "OK, you have to write a report on Native American life in New Mexico. You're great at knowing where to look for information, and you're also good at describing out loud what you've read. Maybe you can read the book, then talk out loud to me and we'll tape it. You can then transcribe it and you'll have your report." By reminding them of what they are good

at, they will begin to focus on their strengths, and can begin to figure out how to use those resources on their own behalf.

Then, each night, I suggest you do the following bedtime ritual. As you put your children to bed, spend at least three minutes of private time, after books and bathroom and teeth-brushing, and ask them to tell you one thing they did that they appreciate themselves for and one thing someone else did that they are thankful for. You can remind them of the things they learned about themselves while doing homework if they are having trouble thinking of something to appreciate in themselves. If you're not there, ask your spouse or the babysitter to perform this ritual with your children. The more you help your children focus on what they appreciate about themselves and those around them, the more they will overflow with optimism, hopefulness, and joy.

Dedicate This Moment

It is better to give than to receive.

—ACTS 20:35

One of the wonderful effects of a sense of gratitude is the desire to spread the joy around. You are
aware you have received something wonderful and,
in a spontaneous upswelling of the heart, want to
give back a measure of the bounty. There are all
kinds of ways to do that, of course, from spontaneous acts of kindness, such as letting in the car that's
trying to nose in ahead of you, to planned giving
through a charitable donation.

But one of my favorite ways is something I
call Dedicate This Moment: When you are enjoying something thoroughly and feeling thankful
to be enjoying it, send the positive energy of that
moment to someone in need. People I know have
sent happy moments dancing to those who are
paralyzed, moments of freedom to those suffering
in prison, and moments of claiming themselves
to those who have been abused. You can send
energy from any positive experience for which you

are grateful. I always ask my friends to send me moments when they are lying on a beach somewhere as I work, and I always send the gratitude I feel at having meaningful work to those who have thankless, boring jobs.

Dedicate This Moment operates on the principle that all of life is connected, and that what happens to one part—say, me—can somehow affect another part—you. It operates a lot like praying for someone; the positive energy generated can actually affect someone else's health and well-being. My favorite verification for the efficacy of prayer is studies that showed people could affect whether or not bacteria and mold grew in petri dishes by praying for them. The bacteria and mold that were prayed for grew more rapidly and prolifically than those that were not.

The effects of positive energy sent across space and time has not yet been studied enough to be accepted fully by the scientific mind. But do we need to wait for proof before giving this a try? After all, it certainly can do no harm, and if we are able to help others feel better through our sense of gratitude, wouldn't that be absolutely wonderful?

Give Thanks for Your Body

Just to be is a blessing. Just to live is holy.
—RABBI ABRAHAM HERSCHEL

This practice is particularly difficult for women, because our relationships with our bodies are fraught
with so much difficulty and dissatisfaction. The
media reinforces such an impossible and singular image for young girls and women to live up to,
and places so much emphasis on appearance, that
virtually none of us—even if we happen to match
the ideal—comes out unscathed. Eating disorders,
plastic surgery, billions spent on make-up and
clothes—we all know the price that is paid. And all
indications are that the obsession is spreading to
boys and men, with calf and biceps implants, hair
replacement, face lifts, and the use of steroids to
build muscle mass on the rise.

Nothing helped me get over this issue more
than a book done by photographer Francis Scavullo,
in which he photographed the world's most beautiful women. There they were, page after page of
breathtaking women, teamed with comments from

the women themselves. Not one of them was satisfied with the way she looked. Everyone complained about something: their nose was too big, hair too thin, mouth too wide. . . . That's when I decided once and for all to stop being dissatisfied with the way I looked. If the world's most beautiful women couldn't be satisfied, no one could, and so I might as well get over myself.

The truth is, no matter what we look like, we are all given bodies that keep us alive, and for that fact alone they are worthy of our appreciation.

My friend Andy Bryner is the best teacher I know of how to live in a body. When he does yoga, he specifically thanks each body part for how it is doing. When he stretches his leg, for example, he says something like, "Thank you, leg, for holding me up so well when I went windsurfing this morning. I appreciate your being able to stretch this much. Perhaps some day you won't be able to go this far, and so today, I really enjoy your ability to go this far." As he stretches, he goes body part by body part, noticing with exquisite particularity what his body has done for him that day and what it is

able to do in this moment, without wishing or hoping it could be different.

You can try the same thing the next time you work out. Or you can do it in bed some evening. Body part by body part, inside and out, give thanks for your incarnation: kidney, liver, lung, stomach; arms, eyes, neck, toes. Think about what each does and how well it does its job.

Honor Your Teachers

No matter what accomplishments you achieve, somebody helped you.

—ALTHEA GIBSON

Who have you most learned from in your life? Your fourth-grade teacher? A college professor? Your spouse? A therapist or friend? All of the above?

No matter who we are or what we have done, as tennis great Althea Gibson reminds us, there have been those who have helped us along the way, someone who said an encouraging word at exactly the right moment, offered an insight that helped

us to get unstuck, or gave us the money we needed to get started. Our culture is so individualistic and competitive that it is easy to forget that we literally accomplish nothing without the help of others.

Sometimes help doesn't come in the way we would like it. Maybe your greatest teachers were those who provided a negative example or provided a mighty obstacle to rebel against. And your greatest teachers aren't necessarily people: some folks have learned most from the animals in their lives; others from great challenge such as a physical disability or illness. Author Carol McClelland, for example, credits her breakdown after the death of her father with her development of a whole new model of change that ultimately became her life's work.

Acknowledging the help we received along the way in our lives—no matter what form it came in—will allow our hearts to soar like a well-tuned orchestra instead of a lonely violin. When we take the time to appreciate those who have been our greatest teachers, we not only express our thanks for the learnings but feel more connected to life as a whole. We see that our lives are a journey on which we become more and more fully who we are

meant to be, and that we are helped on our path by a variety of people and circumstances.

You could, today, spend a few moments thinking about who or what have been your greatest teachers. But what I like to do is to ask the question of a group of people, friends or family gathered around the table for dinner, for example. It's a wonderful way to learn something new about the people in your life—something interesting or profound or moving is always revealed, I've discovered—and to feel connected to one another. And there is something about honoring your teachers out loud, to other people, that really cements the sense of gratefulness and happiness for all you have been given.

Honor Your Ancestors

There is no house like the house of belonging.

—DAVID WHYTE

When I was in college, I used to fantasize that I sprang into life fully formed as a young woman,

like Aphrodite from the seafoam. It was my way of not only repudiating patterns from my parents that I didn't want to replicate, but convincing myself that, in fact, I was incapable of repeating them. It took me decades to acknowledge that while I am indeed my own unique self, I am also the child of my parents, and that indeed I am, for good and bad, more like them than I ever imagined.

It's a paradox. Here we are, a singular, irreplaceable soul here for its own purpose and, at the same time, the somewhat inevitable result of our parents and their physical and emotional legacy. We're the miraculous result of a once-in-a-lifetime meeting of a sperm and an egg, the inheritor of a particular blend of two strands of DNA and a unique personality from not only that DNA, but from all the experiences and training we had from our parents as children, as well as our particular, idiosyncratic reaction to those experiences. And our parents are in the same boat. They are the inheritors, both genetically and circumstantially, from their parents, and their parents from theirs, back throughout time. Thus, in a very real sense, we are the product of all those who came before us.

Because so many of us came from painful or difficult childhood circumstances, it is easy to either deny our connection to those who preceded us or else to blame those circumstances and our relatives for all that goes on in our lives. In either case we get stuck—first, by repeating the past because we fail to acknowledge it; second, by repeating the past because we fail to grow beyond it.

But when we take the time to really give thanks to our ancestors, we place them in their proper context, granting them neither more nor less than their due. We are able to use the lessons they have taught us (even if by negative example) and move beyond their legacy to claim our rightful place in the world. We recognize our deep connection and inhabit fully the "house of belonging."

Dawna Markova has a wonderful practice to make this real for you. "Look in the palm of your hand. Thich Nhat Hanh would say that if you look deeply enough, you'll never be lonely. Each cell of your hand is made from genetic material passed on to you from your mother and father. Whether you adored or despised them, there they are in the palm of your hand. If you look a little deeper, you'll also

see your grandfathers and grandmothers. Deeper still, and there are all your ancestors resting snugly in your DNA. Can you hear them whispering in your ear, 'Maybe this is the one who will carry our dreams into the world, maybe this is the one who will move beyond the limitations that have held us back and carry our dreams into the world.'"

Honoring our connection to those who came before us gives us a sense of belonging and wholeness.

Send Thanksgiving Cards

For more than thirty years, my family has sent Thanksgiving cards rather than Christmas cards to our friends, desiring to spread our gratitude for the many gifts of life.

—JOHN MARKS TEMPLETON

What a great idea! Rather than sending a Christmas card, a holiday letter listing all our accomplishments or a rote greeting, what if we took the time to

catalog the things we are grateful for and tell people about those! Wouldn't it feel wonderful to open
your mailbox and have a card from a friend thanking you for being in her life? Wouldn't it feel great
to be the person who sends such a card?

It doesn't matter what season or event we
choose—Thanksgiving, Christmas, birthdays—only
that we begin to express our feelings of appreciation and gratitude. We all hunger for the connection such heartfelt appreciation creates. Richard
Louv, a columnist for the San Diego *Union Tribune*
and author of *The Web of Life* once wrote a column about a family that, instead of presents, gives
Christmas love letters to one another each year, listing twenty-five reasons why the person receiving
the letter is loved or valued. It is his most widely
requested column, and the idea has been picked up
by a radio station in Los Angeles. "I decided that
my family had better get on board, too," he writes in
The Web of Life.

"My list for Kathy, to whom I have been married
for seventeen years, included: 'You gave birth to
Matthew and Jason. You care deeply about your
patients at work. You're honorable in every part of

your life. I trust you. You don't pick up my socks. You took care of my mother, and me, when she was dying. You go family camping when you'd rather get room service. You introduced me to the joys of room service. You read better books that I do. The scent of your clothes. The way you look when the covers are wrapped around your face....'

"I'm looking forward to giving these lists and to receiving mine. Perhaps your family could try it too. It's just an idea; life's short."

Give Thanks at Meals

Before you taste anything, recite a blessing.
—RABBI AKIVA

As a young girl raised Catholic, I always said grace before eating. After I left the church, however, like many people who have withdrawn from organized religion, I dropped the practice of giving thanks before eating. Since I no longer believed in "God," why should I give thanks? One Thanksgiving, almost twenty-five years later, the impoverishment

of this attitude struck me: Even if there was no God—and by now I was less sure—I was being given something, by farmworkers and grocery clerks and the labors of many others, and I should at least acknowledge that. The result was *A Grateful Heart: Daily Blessings for the Evening Meal from Buddha to the Beatles*. In it, I collected 365 ways to give thanks, many of them not prayers in the traditional sense.

In putting that book together I learned many things. One was how important it was, for me at least, to say something different every day (or almost every day). The problem with the grace from my childhood was that we always said the same one, and therefore, like the Pledge of Allegiance, it lost all its meaning. Variety keeps me awake to meaning.

Mostly I discovered how crucial it is to have a daily ritual of thanksgiving to keep our eyes of appreciation open. It doesn't have to be around eating; many people report that they use *A Grateful Heart* on going to sleep or waking. But the fact that you do it every day at a set time creates a habit of the heart that makes it easier to be thankful all day long.

That being said, I do want to put in a plug for grace before meals, whether you are eating alone or with other people. One of gratitude's most important gifts is fostering a sense of connection. And eating is something that all living things do. When we eat with awareness, with thanksgiving, we strengthen our connection with the rest of life by acknowledging all the living beings that have given their lives so that we might be nourished.

We also strengthen our connection to one another. Rather than sitting in front of a TV, mindlessly shoving food into our mouths, when we sit around a table and say a prayer before eating we connect to one another in our family. We acknowledge that we are sharing this experience, and the acknowledgment itself binds us more firmly together. You can take turns reading something, or speaking spontaneously, or reciting your family's blessing. But whatever you choose to do, when you give thanks before eating, you recognize that you are together, and together, you are a part of something larger than yourselves.

Say "Thank You" as Often as Possible

Let's feel the magic of those two little, big words, "thank you."

—ARDATH RODALE

This practice is very simple. Just say the words "Thank you" as often as possible. Thank you to the toll-taker for taking your money. Thank you to your coworker for bringing in the cookies. Thank you to your friend for calling on a dreary Saturday. That's all—no need to go into a big, long explanation of why you are appreciative. Just a simple, "Thank you."

In truth, this "rote" response we all learned as manners is no small thing. As Daphne Rose Kingma points out in *True Love*, saying, "[Thank you] ... anchors in our minds the fact that we've been given to ... creates an internal attitude of optimism ... and is a character-building act ... [that] develops a positive view of ... the world." In other words, when we say, "Thank you," we are

reminded that we have been given something in this moment, which helps us remember that good things do happen to us and trust that our needs will be provided for in general.

It also has wonderful effects on the people who receive the thank you. It makes them realize that their efforts, whatever they are, have been noticed and appreciated. And we all have a need to be appreciated. Indeed, several people who have worked for me over the years have said that they are at least as much motivated by appreciation as they are by money, and I think that's true for a lot more folks than might admit it.

Saying "Thank you" also goes a long way toward encouraging more of the same behavior in the future. We may not do something to get thanked, but being thanked makes us want to do it again. I realized that recently when I brought roses from my garden into the office and placed one in every person's office. All but one person thanked me, and I notice that my desire to do it again for her is not nearly as strong as it is to do it for everyone else. It's not that I am holding a grudge; my thinking

goes more like this: "If she didn't like it, it makes no sense to do it again."

In a recent article in *Prevention,* Ardath Rodale suggests that readers count the numbers of "Thank you"s they say during one day. I think that's a great idea. So today, count your "Thank you"s. They'll probably increase by virtue of your turning your attention to them.

Leave a Trail of Happiness

[Appreciation] makes immortal all that is best and most beautiful. . . . It exalts the beauty of that which is beautiful. . . . It strips the veil of familiarity from the world, and lays bare and naked sleeping beauty, which is in the spirit of its forms.

—PERCY BYSSHE SHELLEY

Two of the most joy-filled people I know are Joel and Michelle Levey. They seem literally to glow from the inside with the light of vitality and love. One of the greatest things about them is how exquisitely they

give thanks for whatever is done for them. I've seen the letter they sent to their publicist after a recent book tour. They thanked her so eloquently and personally that she cried. When I asked them about the letter, they said they make it a habit to thank in writing people who treat them well. "In our professional corporate work," they write, "we really value the help and support of reliable, qualified, capable people." So they not only let the person know how grateful they are, but they tell the person's boss as well.

As a consequence of such a practice, wherever they go, Joel and Michelle leave a trail of happiness, from the ticket agent at Alaska Airlines; to the waitress who served them with a smile; and the mechanic who fixed their car. Because they try not to take anything for granted, their eyes are open to the gift in the most ordinary situations, and by thanking people for those gifts, they spread the gift around.

You don't necessarily have to send letters (although a card or letter is particularly meaningful to many people, especially these days when the mailbox seems to contain only junk mail and bills). A telephone call or e-mail message will also work.

It's not just strangers and people who do work for you who would appreciate such attention. I know someone who periodically calls up friends and family out of the blue simply to tell them what she appreciates about them. She doesn't do it to get love; she does it out of an overflowing sense of gratitude that they are in her life. And, as you might expect, she is greatly loved as a consequence.

When I think of doing this, I know it's a great idea, but I'm afraid I don't have time to do it (although I feel guilty even admitting that). If you feel the same way, how about trying, after reading this, to send one letter or make one call? I plan to.

Write a "Thank You" to Yourself

It is man's foremost duty to awaken the understanding of the inner Self and to know his own real inner greatness. Once he knows his true worth, he can know the worth of others.

—SWAMI MUKTANANDA

THE PRACTICES OF GRATITUDE

You are amazing, original, the one and only you. You think unique thoughts, express yourself in particular ways, and offer yourself to family and friends in ways that only you can. But I bet you aren't even aware of your beauty, your sensitivity, your quirky outlook on the world. In some ways, it's not possible not to take ourselves for granted—the way we are is just natural to us, and therefore it's hard for us to see just how marvelously wonderful we are.

That's what's so great about friends: they notice what's wonderful and point it out, and suddenly it becomes visible to us too. I'm not even aware, for example, that I have a sense of humor until my friend Rick laughs at something I've said and proclaims, "You're the funniest person I know." Other people may take their kind attentiveness to others for granted, or their creativity, or their precision. Whatever is our own gift, chances are we haven't noticed it.

When we're practicing gratitude, it's easy to notice all the things outside of ourselves we are grateful for—love and friendship and food and laughter—and forget to shine the light of appreciation on ourselves. But we all have splendid qualities,

and if we learn to appreciate ourselves, our sense of gratefulness for our own beings will be magnified and our tendency to notice all our flaws and failings will diminish.

Giving thanks for all our wonderful qualities is one of the ways we learn truly to love ourselves. From that self-love, we can then feel worthy of love from others and have strong, healthy relationships. Because we feel worthy, we can love without being overly demanding, clinging, or rejecting.

Today, try writing a note of thanks to yourself. It can be for anything that you feel grateful to yourself for—being a good friend, for example, or working hard, or dressing with flair. Take the time to think of as many things you are grateful to yourself for as possible. Doesn't it bring a warm smile to your face to think of how marvelous you are?

Fall in Love Again and Again

Choose thy love. Love thy choice.

—GERMAN PROVERB

Why is it that we can be so kind, tolerant, and loving to people we barely know and so demanding, cold, and downright mean to those who are the closest to us? Somehow, by virtue of daily exposure, all the wonderful traits in your beloved that attracted you in the first place become invisible, and every flaw and imperfection looms large. We get so focused on all that we want from our partner but don't have that we can't see the beautiful person who is available to us in this present moment.

I once knew a therapist who claimed that she had discovered a whole new way to improve relationships. Rather than having couples or parents and kids talk out their problems, she claimed that she had better results from having people send a loving, grateful thought to the other person every time they felt themselves getting annoyed or angry. I tried it at home. When I found myself about to

say to my husband, "Why can't you say something interesting?" I would instead focus on something I was grateful for: "I love the way he treats people so gently." What was amazing, was how everything changed. He got more interesting and more loving. Now, whether it was because I changed my attitude and we were not fighting or being caught in hurt feelings, or that my blessing him actually enhanced those qualities in him, I can't say. Nor, frankly, does it matter. The point is that appreciating the good made the good blossom.

Noticing what you love is a mental habit that anyone can learn. Hypnotherapist Milton Erickson used to teach this practice. He said he could get anyone to fall in and out of love with anyone else. All you do is this: Look at a person and find five things you can't stand—for example, their laugh, the way they smell, the way they put down someone, the fact they make a mess when eating, the scum on their teeth. Then find five things you love: the shape of their hands, their big blue eyes, their generosity with material objects, their sense of humor, the way they speak to their kids. For one week, every time

you meet someone, do this practice. Soon you'll discover that you can affect the way you feel toward someone by choosing to focus on what you like.

Then bring this ability home. Become an expert at switching from negative to positive when you find yourself on a mental rant about your mate, and see what happens in your life.

Appreciate Your Kids Just as They Are

Thank you for being.
—TRADITIONAL GREETING OF THE SENECA

As parents, we can get so focused on everything our kids need to learn, to change, to become, that we forget to appreciate them right now for who they are. This is especially true these days, when life is more competitive than ever. We want the best for our children—we want them to have a good education, excel in sports, have friends. We want them to get into a good college, make a good marriage, be wonderful parents of their own. Focused on all

we want for them, we can become preoccupied by their faults, their shortcomings, their lacks. If only Johnny could read better, if only Claudia would sit still, if only Yolanda wasn't so shy. . . .

For the most part, schools help reinforce our fixation on what's wrong, for they have become specialists in diagnosing problems and affixing labels: hyperactive, attention deficit, oppositional, unmotivated. Everyone tells us so much about what's wrong with our kids that it's easy to lose track of our love and appreciation.

My friend Molly has six kids, ranging from twenty-five to eight, all of whom, while very different, have for the most part a healthy sense of self-esteem. Each in his or her own way is blossoming. They do well in school, some better than others. They play sports, some better than others. They have friends, some more than others. They all love one another and their parents a tremendous amount. When I see Molly interact with them, I think I know part of the reason why. She tells them often that they are wonderful just the way they are, that they are loved right now in this moment without changing or improving. No comparing with siblings, no pushing to be better.

What if we greeted our children like the Seneca, saying "Thank you for being" when they woke in the morning or went to sleep at night? What would change for them to feel our gratitude for their being without having to do anything? What would change for us?

Live as if Every Day Is Your Last

Buddha said that fortune changes like the swish of a horse's tail. Tomorrow could be the first day of thirty years of quadriplegia.... The more you open to life the less death becomes the enemy. When you start using death as a means of focusing on life, then everything becomes just as it is, just this moment, an extraordinary opportunity to be really alive.

—STEPHEN LEVINE

Whether it is right or not, sometimes it is only the
possibility of our not being here on Earth anymore
that wakes us up to the beauty of our lives. That's
one of the reasons Buddhists contemplate their
own death—to awaken to the joy that is available in
the present moment.

If this were your last day on Earth, would you
worry about the clutter in your house or the state of
your thighs? I'll bet not. Chances are you'd use the
time to memorize your baby's smile, the smell of
your Sterling Silver roses, the feeling of the rain as
it pelts the top of your head. If this were the last day
on Earth of someone you loved, would you spend
the time arguing about whose turn it is to take out
the garbage or who's right about where to send
your child to school? More likely you'd spend the
time telling him or her how much you love them
and how grateful you are for all they have done
for you.

The truth is, of course, that today might be
our last day on Earth, because the future is never
guaranteed. Too many people go out of the house
blithely one day and never return—victims of car
accidents, heart attacks, drive-by shootings, plane

crashes, and other catastrophes of living—for any of us to take our continued existence for granted.

The purpose of living as if each day were our last is not to create an overwrought sense of having to grab every experience right now. Nor is it an excuse to ignore the garbage that needs to go out, the bills that need to be paid, the clutter that needs to be picked up. Rather it is merely a reminder to be present to our lives as they unfold, to take in, as much as we can, our daily existence.

Thich Nhat Hanh has a wonderful meditation for this, called The Hugging Meditation. It's very simple—all you do is hug someone three times, breathing in and out with awareness. The first time, you both think about how at some time, you don't know when, you will no longer be here. The second time, you focus on how, at some time, you don't know when, the other person will no longer be here. The third time, you truly take in that you are both here now, together in this precious moment.

I try to do it with my husband and daughter whenever I am to be away for any significant length of time, but my new goal is to do it every morning before I walk out the door.

CHAPTER 5

The Deepening Journey

What amazes me is that before we can count we are taught to be grateful for what others do. As we are broken open by our experience, we begin to be grateful for what is, and if we live long enough and deep enough and authentically enough, gratitude becomes a way of life.

—MARK NEPO

By now I hope you've come to experience some of the great joy gratitude can bring, and have begun to see that the attitudes and practices of gratitude lead us on a soul-journey, one that the preceding quote by poet and cancer survivor Mark Nepo so perfectly describes. Gratitude begins with training in what we call manners, a learned response to being on the receiving end of a human transaction: "Mrs. Smith just gave you a cookie, Janey. Now what do you say?" Despite the benefits of such thanks, they are contingent on someone doing something specific for us, and while many of us remain at this level of gratitude, our souls call out for us to move to a deeper level.

Here we begin to discover gratitude apart from a specific human giver, apart from roses on Valentine's Day and the CD player on Christmas, and acknowledge the gift of life itself. Here we begin to be appreciative of everything, as teachers along our soul's path. This second level of gratitude is most often found through suffering, by choosing to get soft and wide, rather than rigid and pointy, under the yoke of life's difficulties. When we allow ourselves to be broken open by life rather than

broken down by it, we begin to be grateful for the difficulties themselves—to cancer for bringing us to our feelings; to bankruptcy for saving us from the rat race; to a demanding person for teaching us how to stand up for ourselves.

When we live from this place long enough, we begin actually to inhabit gratitude, our every inhalation and exhalation a breath of thanksgiving no matter what is going on in the external world. Not many travelers make it all the way here permanently; this is the territory of saints. But all of us experience this spot in glimpses, moments in which we look up at the sky and see it for the work of art that it is; hear Beethoven's Ninth and feel the majestic surprise of such music in our lives; feel our baby's pudgy fingers on our face and cry tears of thanks for her being.

At each level of gratitude, our soul's capacity deepens. At the first level, we experience contentment—we wanted a cookie and we got it. At the second, we experience meaning—we're here for a purpose and are therefore grateful for all of life's lessons. At the third, we dwell in pure joy, "the simple response of our heart to this given life in all its fullness," as Brother David Steindl-Rast puts it.

May you experience all the levels of thankfulness and the soul-gifts that each offers. For then it will be truly possible to give and receive joy every day of your life.

The Top 12 Ways to Bring More Gratefulness into Your Life

Practice daily—in a journal, in an email to a gratitude partner, when you're driving home from work, at dinner with your family, before going to sleep. The more you create a routine, the easier it will be to remember.

Create visual or auditory reminders—a sign, a popup on your computer, reminders sent to your cell phone (sign up at *wellsphere.com*).

Focus on what's right in your life instead of what's wrong.

Say "thank you" to others as often as possible.

Make sure to include yourself. What did you do well today? What are you thankful to yourself for? The

more we appreciate ourselves, the more our good qualities grow.

Especially when they're annoying or frustrating you, remember why you love your spouse, kids, and friends.

Compare well—when you find yourself envying someone, focus on what you do have that other people don't.

Give thanks for your body. What can you appreciate about it right now?

Have a gratitude rock—a little pebble you carry in your pocket. Every time you feel it, think of something you are thankful for.

When difficult things happen, ask yourself: What's right about this? Yes, it's awful, but if something were right about it, what would it be?

Look for the hidden blessings in challenges. How have you grown?

Imagine that this day is the first and last of your life. How would you treasure it?

About the Author

Photo credit: Sunshine Design Studio

Inspirational author and international coach, M. J. Ryan is one of the creators of *The New York Times* best-selling *Random Acts of Kindness* series and the author of *The Happiness Makeover* (finalist in the 2005 Books for Better Living award), *This Year I Will...*, *The Power of Patience*, *Trusting Yourself*, *The Giving Heart*, and *365 Health and Happiness Boosters*, among other titles.

Dubbed "an expert in human fulfillment," she specializes in coaching high performance executives, entrepreneurs, and leadership teams around the world. Her work is based on a combination of positive psychology, strengths-based coaching, the wisdom traditions, and cutting-edge brain research. She is a member of the International Coaching Federation, with corporate, government, and non-

profit clients. She has appeared on *The Today Show*, CNN, and hundreds of radio programs. Articles on her work have appeared in *The New York Times*, *USA Today*, *The Wall Street Journal*, *Health*, *Family Circle*, *Ladies' Home Journal*, *Town and Country*, *Cosmopolitan*, and *Yoga Journal*.

M. J. gives speeches and workshops throughout the country, including with Marianne Williamson at the Marble Collegiate Church in New York, the Alliance for the New Humanity with Deepak Chopra, Peeke Week Retreats with Pamela Peeke, the Oceans of Gratitude cruise, Thanksgiving Square in Dallas, the Crossroads Center in Chicago, the Kripalu Center for Yoga and Health in Massachusetts, Esalen Institute at Big Sur, Robert Redford's Sundance resort in Utah, and A Woman's Way retreat center in Sedona. She lives in the San Francisco Bay Area with her family. Visit her online at *www.mj-ryan.com*.

To Our Readers

Conari Press, an imprint of Red Wheel/Weiser, publishes books on topics ranging from spirituality, personal growth, and relationships to women's issues, parenting, and social issues. Our mission is to publish quality books that will make a difference in people's lives—how we feel about ourselves and how we relate to one another. We value integrity, compassion, and receptivity, both in the books we publish and in the way we do business.

Our readers are our most important resource, and we value your input, suggestions, and ideas about what you would like to see published. Please feel free to contact us, to request our latest book catalog, or to be added to our mailing list.

Conari Press
An imprint of Red Wheel/Weiser, LLC
665 Third Street, Suite 400
San Francisco, CA 94107
www.redwheelweiser.com